*Philosophy of Language*

# PHILOSOPHY OF LANGUAGE

FOUNDATIONS OF PHILOSOPHY SERIES

*William P. Alston*

*University of Michigan*

**PRENTICE-HALL, INC.** ENGLEWOOD CLIFFS, N. J.

**PHILOSOPHY OF LANGUAGE, Alston**

FOUNDATIONS OF PHILOSOPHY SERIES

C-66379

Current printing (last digit):
12

PRENTICE-HALL INTERNATIONAL, INC., London

PRENTICE-HALL OF AUSTRALIA, PTY., LTD., Sydney

PRENTICE-HALL OF CANADA, LTD., Toronto

PRENTICE-HALL OF INDIA (PRIVATE) LTD., New Delhi

PRENTICE-HALL OF JAPAN, INC., Tokyo

PRENTICE-HALL DE MEXICO, S.A., Mexico City

*To Valerie*

without whom not

# FOUNDATIONS

# OF PHILOSOPHY

Many of the problems of philosophy are of such broad relevance to human concerns, and so complex in their ramifications, that they are, in one form or another, perennially present. Though in the course of time they yield in part to philosophical inquiry, they may need to be rethought by each age in the light of its broader scientific knowledge and deepened ethical and religious experience. Better solutions are found by more refined and rigorous methods. Thus, one who approaches the study of philosophy in the hope of understanding the best of what it affords will look for both fundamental issues and contemporary achievements.

Written by a group of distinguished philosophers, the Foundations of Philosophy Series aims to exhibit some of the main problems in the various fields of philosophy as they stand at the present stage of philosophical history.

While certain fields are likely to be represented in most introductory courses in philosophy, college classes differ widely in emphasis, in method of instruction, and in rate of progress. Every instructor needs freedom to change his course as his own philosophical interests, the size and makeup of his classes, and the needs of his students vary from year to year. The thirteen volumes in the Foundations of Philosophy Series—each complete in itself, but complementing the others—offer a new flexibility to the instructor, who can create his own textbook by combining several volumes as he wishes, and can choose different combinations at different times. Those volumes that are not used in an introductory course will be found valuable, along with other texts or collections of readings, for the more specialized upper-level courses.

ELIZABETH BEARDSLEY        MONROE BEARDSLEY

# PREFACE

Though the philosophy of language might reasonably be thought of as comprising anything that philosophers do when they think, *qua* philosophers, about language, I have not attempted a survey of that heterogeneous field of activity. Instead, I have presented the philosophy of language in one of its guises, as an attempt to get clear about the basic concepts we use in thinking about language. (This contrasts with thinking of the philosophy of language as an attempt to exhibit language as one of the forms of the world spirit, or as an attempt to provide an over-all synthesis of conclusions about language, arrived at in the various social sciences.) As so conceived, the philosopher of language tries to determine, for example, what language is and how it is related to more or less analogous forms of activity (Chapter 3), what it is for a linguistic expression to be meaningful (Chapter 4), what it is for a linguistic expression to have a certain meaning (Chapters 1 and 2), what it is for a linguistic expression to be vague or to be used metaphorically (Chapter 5). I have chosen to proceed primarily by discussing these problems according to my lights, rather than by enumerating and classifying alternative positions, though I hope that my discussion has maintained contact with many of the significant ideas to be found in the literature. With respect to what I take to be the central problem, "What is it for a linguistic expression to have a certain meaning?", I have devoted almost all of the first chapter to a critical review of the most prominent positions. I should also add that I have approached these problems in a relatively informal manner, in contrast with logistically minded theorists, like Carnap, who seek illumination by the construction of formalized schemata for simplified languages.

I am extremely indebted to the editors of this series, Monroe and Elizabeth Beardsley, and to William Frankena and George Nakhnikian, as well as to my wife, Valerie, all of whom read the manuscript in an early and overinflated form and made many helpful suggestions. More generally, I am indebted to all those students and colleagues with whom I have discussed semantical topics over the years, particularly Richard and Helen Cartwright, Paul Henle, Julius Moravcsik, Kenneth Pike, John Searle, J. O. Urmson, Paul Ziff, and most particularly David Shwayder, with whom ideas about language have been exchanged to the point that only considerations of charity inhibit me from attributing the whole production to him. Finally, I should like to express appreciation to Mrs. Alice Gantt for prompt and expert typing.

WILLIAM P. ALSTON

# CONTENTS

# INTRODUCTION

The philosophy of language is even less well-defined and less in possession of a clear principle of unity than most other branches of philosophy. The problems concerning language that are typically dealt with by philosophers constitute a loosely knit collection, for which it is difficult to find any clear criterion separating it from problems concerning language dealt with by grammarians, psychologists, and anthropologists. We can get an initial sense of the range of this collection by surveying the various points within philosophy at which a concern with language emerges.

**Sources of the philosopher's concern with language: metaphysics** First, consider the ways in which problems concerning language crop up in the various branches of philosophy. Metaphysics is a part of philosophy roughly characterizable as an attempt to formulate the most general and pervasive facts about the world, including an enumeration of the most basic categories to which entities belong and some depiction of their interrelations. There have always been philosophers who have tried to get at some of these fundamental facts by considering the fundamental features of the language we use to talk about the world. In Book X of Plato's *Republic*, we find him saying, "Whenever a number of individuals have a common name, we assume them to have also a corresponding idea or form." (596) To spell out this rather cryptic remark, Plato is calling our attention to a pervasive feature of language, that a given common noun or adjective, for example, 'tree' or 'sharp,' can be truly applied in the same sense to a large number of different individual things; his position is that this is possible only if there exists some one entity named by the general term in question—treeness, sharpness—of which each of the individuals partakes. If this were not the case, it would be impossible for the general term to be applied in the same sense to a number of different individuals.

Again, we find Aristotle in his *Metaphysics* arguing as follows:

> And so one might even raise the question whether the words 'to walk,' 'to be healthy,' 'to sit,' imply that each of these things is existent, and similarly in other cases of this sort; for none of them is either self-subsistent or capable of being separated from substance, but rather, if anything, it is that which walks or sits or is healthy that is an existent thing. Now these are seen to be more real because there is something definite which underlies them (i.e., the substance or individual) which is implied in such a predicate; for we never use the word 'good' or 'sitting' without implying this. (Book Zeta, Chapter 1)

Here Aristotle starts from the fact that we do not use verbs except in connection with subjects, that we do not go around saying 'Sits,' 'Walks,' etc., but rather, 'He is sitting," or 'She is walking.' From this fact he concludes that substances, "things," have an independent kind of existence in a way that actions do not, that substances are more fundamental ontologically than actions.

A more outré example can be found in the late nineteenth century German philosopher, Meinong, who started with the assumption that every meaningful expression in a sentence (at least any meaningful expression that has the function of referring to something) must have a referent; otherwise, there would be nothing for it to mean. Hence, when we have an obviously meaningful expression that refers to nothing in the real world, for example, 'the Fountain of Youth,' in the sentence, 'De Soto was searching for the Fountain of Youth,' we must suppose that it refers to a "subsistent" entity, which does not *exist* but has some other mode of being. This doctrine, as well as the Platonic position presented above, is based on a confused assimilation of meaning and reference, which we shall try to straighten out in the first chapter.

The assumption behind these patterns of metaphysical argumentation has been made quite explicit in the twentieth century philosophical movement known as logical atomism, the most distinguished exponents of which have been Bertrand Russell and Ludwig Wittgenstein (in his earlier period). In Russell's series of articles, "The Philosophy of Logical Atomism," he makes the principle quite explicit.

> . . . in a logically correct symbolism there will always be a certain fundamental identity of structure between a fact and the symbol for it; and . . . the complexity of the symbol corresponds very closely with the complexity of the facts symbolized by it.[1]

[1] *Logic and Knowledge,* ed. R. C. Marsh (London: George Allen & Unwin, Ltd., 1956).

Note that this identity of structure is postulated to hold not between any existing language and the basic metaphysical structure of the world, but only between a "logically perfect language" and the metaphysical structure. The assumption is that when we have devised such a language, or have acquired at least a sketchy idea of what such a language would be like, we will then be able to draw various conclusions concerning the types of facts of which reality is made and the structure of each of these facts. We will ascertain what different types of sentences we have in that language for asserting facts, for example, simple subject-predicate sentences like 'This book is heavy' and existential sentences like 'There is a cat on the porch'; and we will see how these various types of sentences are logically related. This will tell us what the basic sorts of facts are of which reality is made and how facts of these various sorts are interrelated.

**Logic**    Another branch of philosophy in which concern with language becomes prominent is logic. Logic is the study of inference, more precisely the attempt to devise criteria for separating valid from invalid inferences. Since reasoning is carried on in language, the analysis of inferences depends on an analysis of the statements that figure as premises and conclusions. A study of logic reveals the fact that the validity or invalidity of an inference depends on the forms of the statements that make up the premises and conclusion, where by 'form' is meant the kinds of terms the statements contain and the way in which these terms are combined in the statement. Thus, of two inferences that superficially look very much alike, one may be valid and the other invalid because of a difference in the form of one or more of the statements involved. Consider the following pair of inferences.

1.    Joe Carpenter sells insurance in our town.
      Joe Carpenter belongs to the First Methodist Church.
      ▸ Therefore, Joe Carpenter both sells insurance in our town and belongs to the First Methodist Church.
2.    Someone sells insurance in our town.
      Someone belongs to the First Methodist Church.
      ▸ Therefore, someone both sells insurance in our town and belongs to the First Methodist Church.

Now 1 is clearly a valid argument, and 2 is clearly invalid. Given the facts that *someone* sells insurance in this town and that *someone* belongs to the First Methodist Church, it does not at all follow that there is anyone of whom both these things are true. Since one of these arguments is valid and the other invalid, it must be that despite superficial grammatical similarities, a sentence like *a.* 'Joe Carpenter sells insurance in our town' is of a very different logical form from a sentence like *b.* 'Someone sells insurance in our town.' There are other indications of this. Sentence *b* is equivalent to 'There is someone who sells insurance in our town' and to 'The class of persons who sell insurance in our town is not empty,' but we can find no such equivalents for sentence *a.* When the premises and conclusion of inference 2 are put into one of these forms, the argument loses its superficial resemblance to inference 1 and does not look valid at all.

3.    There is someone who sells insurance in our town.
      There is someone who belongs to the First Methodist Church.
      ▶ Therefore, there is someone who both sells insurance in our town and belongs to the First Methodist Church.

It is clear from such examples that an important part of logic consists in a classification of statements in terms of their "logical" form (that is, aspects of form that are relevant to the evaluation of inference). And this classification in turn requires a classification of the types of terms that enter into statements, for a difference in form quite often rests upon a difference in the types of terms involved. In the preceding example, the difference in logical form between sentences *a* and *b* rests upon a fundamental difference between a proper name like 'Joe Carpenter,' which has the function of picking out a particular individual, and a locution like 'someone,' which has quite a different function.

**Epistemology**    The branch of philosophy known as *Epistemology* or *Theory of Knowledge* becomes concerned with language at a number of points, the most prominent of which is the problem of a priori knowledge. We have "a priori" knowledge when we know something to be the case without this knowledge being grounded on experience. It seems that we have knowledge of this sort in mathematics, and perhaps in other areas as well; and the fact that we do have such knowledge has often seemed puzzling to philosophers. How is it that we are able to know with certainty, apart from observation, measurement, etc., that the angles of a Euclidian triangle all together equal 180 degrees, and that 8 plus 7 always and invariably equals 15? How can we be sure that no experience will ever falsify these convictions? One answer that has often been given is that in such cases what we are asserting is true by definition, or true by virtue of the meanings of the terms involved. That is, it is part of what we mean by '8,' '7,' '15,' 'plus,' and 'equals,' that 8 plus 7 equals 15; and to deny this statement seriously would involve changing the meaning of one or more of these terms. The adequacy of this account of a priori knowledge is and has been the subject of considerable controversy; but whether or not the position is justified, it is clear that even in taking it seriously, we are inevitably led into questions concerning what it is for a term to have a certain meaning and how a statement can be *true* by reason of the fact that certain terms have the meaning they do.

**Reform of**     There are also philosophical motives for concern with language,
**language**     which have to do not with the problems of one or another branch
of philosophy but with kinds of activity into which philosophers are typically led in many branches of the subject. One of these is the reform of language. Thinkers in many fields are given to complaining about the deficiencies of language, but philosophers have been more preoccupied with this sort of problem than most, and for good reason. Philosophy is a much more purely verbal activity than is a science that collects facts about chemical reactions, social structures, or rock formations. Verbal discussion is the philosopher's laboratory, in which he puts his ideas to the test. It is not surprising that the philosopher should be especially sensitive to flaws in his major instrument. Philosophical complaints about language have taken many forms. There are the philosophers of mystical intuition, such as Plotinus and Bergson, who regard language as such to be unsuitable for the formulation of fundamental truth. From this standpoint, one can really apprehend truth only by some wordless union with reality; linguistic formulations give us at best only more or less distorted perspectives. But more often philosophers have not been willing to abjure talking, even in theory. Complaints have usually been levelled against some current state or condition of language, and the implication is that steps could be taken to remedy this condition. These philosophers can usefully be divided into two groups. There are those who hold that "ordinary language," the language of everyday discourse, is perfectly suitable for philosophical purposes, and that the mischief lies in deviating from ordinary language without really providing any way of attaching sense to the deviation. We find examples of this sort of complaint here and there in the history of philosophy, for example, in Locke's complaints against scholastic jargon; however, it is in our own day that such complaints have become the basis of a philosophical movement, "ordinary language philosophy." In its strongest form, as we find it in the later work of Ludwig Wittgenstein, it maintains that all, or at least most, of the problems of philosophy stem from the fact that philosophers have misused certain crucial terms, such as 'know,' 'see,' 'free,' 'true,' and 'reason.' It is because philosophers have departed from the ordinary use(s) of these terms without putting anything intelligible in their place that they have fallen into insoluble puzzles over whether we can know what other people are thinking or feeling, whether we ever really directly see any physical object, whether anyone ever acts freely, and

whether we ever have any reason to suppose that things will happen in one way rather than another in the future. According to Wittgenstein, the role of the philosopher who has seen this point is that of a therapist; his job is to remove the "conceptual cramps" into which we have fallen.

Second, there are those who hold, by contrast, that the trouble comes from the fact that ordinary language itself is inadequate for philosophical purposes, by reason of its vagueness, inexplicitness, ambiguity, context-dependence, and misleadingness. These philosophers, such as Leibniz, Russell, and Carnap, see as their task the construction of an artificial language, or at least the adumbration of such a language, in which these defects will be remedied. As was pointed out previously, this enterprise is sometimes enlivened by the conviction that from the structure of such a language one can read off basic facts about the metaphysical structure of reality.

For our purposes, the main interest of these complaints and schemes for reform lies in the way in which general conceptions of language and meaning are involved in them. Even the mystical position presupposes some notion of the nature of language; otherwise, one could have no basis for holding language as such to be incapable of serving as an adequate formulation of truth. The other positions necessarily involve more positive conceptions of the conditions under which language is meaningful and is performing its functions adequately. Thus, the verifiability criterion of meaningfulness, to which we shall devote most of a chapter, grows out of a position of the sort last discussed.

**Philosophy as analysis**   The final point concerns the notion that the primary, if not the whole, job of philosophy is conceptual analysis. The analysis of basic concepts has always been a major concern of philosophers. In the Dialogues of Plato, Socrates is represented as spending a great deal of his time asking questions like "What is justice?" and "What is knowledge?" Aristotle's works are, in large part, concerned with attempts to arrive at adequate definitions of terms like 'cause,' 'good,' 'motion,' and 'know.' Traditionally, it has been felt that however important this activity was, it was still a preliminary to the ultimate tasks of the philosopher—those of arriving at an adequate conception of the basic structure of the world and an adequate set of standards for human conduct and social organization. But in our time there has been a growing conviction that the method used in philosophy, which may be briefly defined as armchair reflection unsupplemented by special observation or experimentation, does not really suffice to yield any substantive conclusions concerning the nature of the world or the conditions under which life is lived well or ill, and that what it *is* fitted to produce is clarity and explicitness with respect to the basic concepts in terms of which we think about the world and human life. This massive shift in the center of gravity of philosophical activity is of particular relevance to the philosophy of language because of an accompanying shift in the conception of conceptual analysis itself. There are three importantly different ways of formulating a problem in analytical philosophy, whether we are dealing with causation, truth, knowledge, or moral obligation. To take the problem of knowledge for our model, we can say that 1. we are investigating the nature of knowledge, 2. we are analyzing the concept of knowledge, or 3. we are trying to make explicit what one is saying when he says that he knows something to be the case. 1 and 2 are likely to be misleading methodologically. 1 suggests, falsely, that the task is one of locating and inspecting some entity called 'knowledge,' an entity that exists and is what it is independent of our thought and discourse. Unfortunately, no one has ever provided an acceptable technique for locating and examining such entities. 2 is apt to be misleading unless it is recognized to be simply an alternative form of 3, for it suggests that the task is one of introspectively scrutinizing something called a concept and discovering the parts of which it consists and the way they are put together. Again, it does not seem to be possible to develop an objective technique for doing any such thing. The realization has grown that even when a philosopher dealing with knowledge formulates his problem as 1 or 2, what he really does, insofar as his results have any value, is to reflect on various features of the use of 'know' and its cognates.

Thus to the extent that philosophy consists of conceptual analysis, it is always concerned with language. And if it is either all or a large part of the philosopher's business to bring out features of the use or meaning of various words and forms of statement, it is essential for him to proceed on the basis of some general conception of the nature of linguistic use and meaning. This becomes especially important when analytical philosophers become involved in persistent disputes over what a given word means, or over whether two expressions or forms of expression have the same or different meaning. There are serious disagreements in analytical philosophy over whether 'I know that $p$' means the same as 'I believe that $p$, I have adequate grounds for this belief, and $p$ is the case'; whether 'A is the cause of B' means simply that A and B are, in fact, regularly conjoined; whether 'feels sad' means the same in 'I feel sad' and 'He feels sad'; and whether any theoretical statement in science can have the same meaning as some combination of reports of observation. When such disputes are not settled by our intuitive sense of what linguistic expressions mean, the philosopher is forced to develop some explicit theory of what it is for a linguistic expression to have a certain meaning and of the conditions under which two expressions will have the same meaning. Thus, insofar as philosophy is thought of primarily as conceptual analysis, the philosophy of language occupies a central position in the theory of philosophical method.

**Problems of the philosophy of language**    Having seen some of the points in the more central portions of philosophy at which one is naturally led to an explicit consideration of problems concerning language, we can proceed to a brief preliminary survey of these problems. As I pointed out earlier, it would be unrealistic to expect a tight unity in this subject. But if we can agree to regard conceptual analysis as the heart of philosophy, we can give pride of place among these problems to the task of providing an adequate analysis of the basic concepts we use in thinking about language. Although there is no reason why a philosopher should not put his analytical tools to work on any of the basic concepts dealing with language, the tendency has been to concentrate on semantic concepts, for example, the concept of linguistic meaning and its cognates, sameness of meaning, meaningfulness, etc. This has been partly because many of the philosophical concerns enumerated in the first part of this introduction naturally lead one to raise questions about the nature of meaning, and partly because the fact that a given word has a certain meaning is apt to appear mysterious in the way that often gives rise to philosophical reflection. A large part of this book will be concerned with the analysis of semantic concepts.

It would be misleading to suggest that the philosophy of language, even as practiced by analytical philosophers, is restricted to conceptual analysis, to clarifying the basic concepts dealing with language. There are a number of other tasks which philosophers typically set themselves. There is the classification of linguistic acts, of "uses" or "functions" of language, of types of vagueness, of types of terms, of various sorts of metaphor. There are discussions of the role of metaphor in extending language; of the interrelations of language, thought, and culture; and of the peculiarities of poetic, religious, and moral discourse. Proposals are made for constructing artificial languages for various purposes. There are detailed investigations of the peculiarities of particular sorts of expressions, such as proper names and plural referring expressions, and particular grammatical forms, such as the subject-predicate form. Some of these problems lie in the borderland between philosophy and more special disciplines, and all of them might be dealt with in one or another of these disciplines. Thus, psychology might take on the job of distinguishing between different sorts of linguistic behavior, and descriptive linguistics could be expected to provide classifications of types of expressions. But if these problems belong in principle to the more special disciplines, they belong to their foundations; and philosophy has traditionally had much traffic with high level problems in the sciences, especially when these sciences are in early stages of construction. I shall have something to say about some of these problems.

This book is written from a certain philosophical orientation— that roughly indicated by the term 'analytical philosophy.' There is a great deal of philosophizing about language that is carried on from very different standpoints, and there the problems take on quite different shapes. It is neither possible nor desirable in a volume of this size to survey all the philosophical approaches to language. By way of compensation, I have included in the bibliography some suggestions for reading in other approaches.

# THEORIES OF MEANING

# 1

**The problem**
**of meaning** The present chapter is concerned with the nature of linguistic meaning. This is a problem of philosophical analysis, which is best formulated as follows: "What are we saying about a linguistic expression when we specify its meaning?" [1] That is, we are trying to give an adequate characterization of one of the uses of 'mean' and its cognates.

There are many other uses of 'mean,' some of which might be confused with our sense.

1. That is no mean accomplishment. (insignificant)
2. He was so mean to me. (cruel)
3. I mean to help him if I can. (intend)
4. The pasage of this bill will mean the end of second class citizenship for vast areas of our population. (result in)
5. Once again life has meaning for me. (significance)
6. What is the meaning of this? (explanation)
7. He just lost his job. That means that he will have to start writing letters of application all over again. (implies)

In these cases we are talking about people, actions, events, or situations rather than about words, phrases, or sentences. The cases in which we apply, or seem to apply, 'means' to a linguistic expression, but where 'mean' does not have the sense we are examining are rare; but it is here that confusion is most likely to occur.

---

[1] Although this is the canonical form, I shall not hesitate to employ the other forms, "What is linguistic meaning?" and "How is the concept of linguistic meaning to be analyzed?" as stylistic variants. (See p.7.)

8. Keep off the grass. This means you.

Here it seems plausible to regard 'this' as referring to the sentence, 'Keep off the grass.' But it is clear that we are *not* saying what the sentence means. An English-French phrase book would not contain the entry: Keep off the grass—*vous.* This is the use in which 'mean' means very much the same as 'refer.' It is more commonly used of people, as in "Who do you mean?"—"I mean Susie." But, as in 8, it can be used of linguistic expressions. Again consider:

9. Lucky Strike means fine tobacco.

Here we are not talking about a linguistic expression, although it may seem at first sight as if we are. We are not giving the meaning of the phrase, 'Lucky Strike.' No dictionary could possibly contain such an entry. (If *Webster's* did contain this entry, the American Tobacco Company would undoubtedly be delighted.) This is an example of the same use we have in:

That look on his face means trouble.
When he begins complaining, that means he is getting better.

In all these cases, we are saying that one thing or event is a reliable indication of the existence of another.

There is one sense in which we all know perfectly well what we are saying when we say what a word means. We succeed in communicating with each other by saying things like " 'Procrastinate' means *put things off*," [2] "He doesn't know what 'suspicious' means," and so on. In general, we know how to support, attack, and test such statements, we know when such statements are warranted and when they are not, we know what practical implications accepting such a statement would have, and so on. What we lack, in advance of a philosophical investigation, is an explicit and coherent account of these abilities.

**Types of theories of meaning**  The literature on this subject contains a bewildering diversity of approaches, conceptions, and theories, most of which can be grouped into three types, which I shall call 'referential,' 'ideational,' and 'behavioral.' The referential theory identifies the meaning of an expression with that to which it refers or with the referential connection, the ideational theory with the ideas with which it

---

[2] A word about the notation. We shall regularly italicize what follows 'means' in 'E means. . . .' (or what follows 'is' in 'The meaning of E is. . . .') This is intended to reflect the fact that when expressions are put into this slot, they have a unique kind of occurrence, for which we shall use the term 'exhibit.' (See p. 21.)

is associated, and the behavioral theory with the stimuli that evoke its utterance and/or the responses that it in turn evokes. Each of these kinds of theory exists in more forms than I shall have time to consider. But I shall try to choose forms of each that will clearly exemplify its basic features.

**The
referential
theory**
The referential theory has been attractive to a great many theorists because it seems to provide a simple answer that is readily assimilable to natural ways of thinking about the problem of meaning. It has seemed to many that proper names have an ideally transparent semantic structure. Here is the word 'Fido'; there is the dog the word names. Everything is out in the open; there is nothing hidden or mysterious. Its having the meaning it has is simply constituted by the fact that it is the name of that dog.[3] It is both tempting and natural to suppose that a similar account can be given for all meaningful expressions. It is thought that every meaningful expression names something or other, or at least stands to something or other in a relation something like naming (designating, labelling, referring to, etc.). The something or other referred to does not have to be a particular concrete, observable thing like Fido. It could be a kind of thing (as with "common names" like 'dog'), a quality ('perseverance'), a state of affairs ('anarchy'), a relationship ('owns'), and so on. But the supposition is that for any meaningful expression, we can understand what it is for it to have a certain meaning by noting that there is something or other to which it refers. "Words all have meaning, in the simple sense that they are symbols that stand for something other than themselves." [4]

The referential theory exists in a more and a less naïve version. Both versions subscribe to the statement that for an expression to have a meaning is for it to refer to something other than itself, but they locate meaning in different areas of the situation of reference. The more naïve view is that the meaning of an expression is that to which the expression refers; [5] the more sophisticated view is that the meaning of the expression is to be identified with the relation between the expres-

[3] A more penetrating account of proper names would show that this is a singularly unfortunate model for an account of meaning. It is questionable whether proper names can be correctly said to have meaning. They are not assigned meanings in dictionaries. One who does not know what 'Fido' is the name of is not thereby deficient in his grasp of English in the way he would be if he did not know what 'dog' means. And the fact that 'Fido' is used in different circles as the name of a great many different dogs does not show that it has a great many different meanings or that it is a highly ambiguous word.

[4] Bertrand Russell, *Principles of Mathematics* (London: Cambridge University Press, 1903), p. 47.

[5] It is difficult to find a full-blown presentation of this version in the works of reputable philosophers. But since it exercises an enormous influence on popular thinking about language, it is worth-while to exhibit its defects.

sion and its referent, that the referential connection constitutes the meaning.

The first form of the theory can easily be shown to be inadequate by virtue of, the fact that two expressions can have different meanings but the same referent. Russell's classic example of this point concerns 'Sir Walter Scott' and 'the author of *Waverley*.' These two expressions refer to the same individual, since Scott is the author of *Waverley*, but they do not have the same meaning. If they did, the statement that Scott is the author of *Waverley* would be known to be true just by knowing the meaning of the constituent terms. It is a fundamental principle that whenever two referring expressions have the same meaning, for example, 'my only uncle' and 'the only brother either of my parents has,' then the identity statement with these terms as components, "My only uncle is the only brother either of my parents has," is necessarily true just by virtue of the meanings of these expressions. But this is not the case with "Scott is the author of *Waverley*." This statement is a particularly good example because the identity of the author of these novels was at first kept secret, so that many people could understand the sentence 'Scott is the author of *Waverley*' (Scott was already a famous poet) without knowing whether it was true. In general, anything to which we can refer can be referred to by many expressions that do not have the same meaning at all, for example, John F. Kennedy can be referred to as 'the President of the U.S.A. in 1962,' 'the U.S. President assassinated in Dallas.' Such examples show that it cannot simply be the fact that an expression refers to a certain object that gives it the particular meaning it has.

The converse phenomenon—same meaning but different referents—can be demonstrated, not for different expressions, but for different utterances of the same expression. There is a class of terms, sometimes called "indexical terms," for example, 'I,' 'you,' 'here,' 'this,' which systematically change their reference with changes in the conditions of their utterance. When Jones utters the word 'I,' it refers to Jones; when Smith utters it, it refers to Smith. But this fact doesn't mean that 'I' has different meanings corresponding to these differences. If a word like 'I' had a distinguishable meaning for every person to whom it has ever been used to refer, it would be the most ambiguous word in English. Think of how many different meanings we would have to learn before we could be said to have mastered the use of the word; in fact, every time a new speaker of English learned to use the word, it would acquire a new meaning. But this is fantastic. The word has a single meaning—*the speaker*. And it is because it always has this meaning that its referent systematically varies with variations in the conditions of utterance.

**Do all**
**meaningful**
**expressions**
**refer to**
**something?**
Because of these readily appreciable difficulties, the more careful versions of the referential theory take the second alternative. Even though Russell, for example, often talks as if the meaning of an expression *is* what it stands for, we also find him saying things like: "When we ask what constitutes meaning, . . . we are asking, not who is the individual meant, but what is the relation of the word to the individual which makes the one mean the other." [6] This version cannot be disposed of by pointing out that reference and meaning do not always vary together. For it may be that although 'Scott' and 'the author of *Waverley*' refer to the same person, they are not related to that referent in the same way, though it is difficult to say whether they are until we have some account of the sort of relation in question. But at this point a more fundamental difficulty comes into view. No sort of referential theory will be adequate as a general account of meaning unless it is true that all meaningful linguistic expressions do refer to something. And if we take a careful look at the matter, it will be seen that this is not the case.

First of all, there are conjunctions and other components of language, which serve an essentially connective function. Do words like 'and,' 'if,' 'is,' and 'whereas' refer to anything? It seems not. Referential theorists usually reply to this objection by denying that "syncategorematic" [7] terms like these have meaning "in isolation," or that they have meaning in the primary sense in which nouns, adjectives, and verbs have meaning. It is possible, of course, that in the end we may be driven to the position that there is no one sense in which all linguistic units to which we ordinarily assign meaning, have meaning. But to admit this before we have made an earnest effort to find a single sense would be a counsel of despair. It certainly seems that in saying " 'Procrastinate' means *put things off*" and " 'If' means *provided that*" we are saying things which, in some important respect, are the same sort of thing; we are, so to say, speaking in the same logical tone of voice. And we should not lightly give up the attempt to spell out explicitly what is common.

Moreover, the idea that every meaningful linguistic expression refers to something encounters rough going even in those stretches of language where the referential theorist feels most secure. Proponents of this theory generally take it as obvious that nouns like 'pencil,' adjec-

---

[6] *Analysis of Mind* (London: George Allen & Unwin, 1921), p. 191.

[7] This term was introduced by medieval logicians to apply to words like conjunctions, which were regarded as not standing for anything and so as not having meaning "in isolation." These were the linguistic units that were left over after one had gone through everything that could be assigned to Aristotle's ten "Categories," a classification of terms made by Aristotle. Thus, the remnants were terms that were used only *with* (syn—categorematic) the categories.

tives like 'courageous,' and verbs like 'run' refer to something or other. It is not always recognized that it is sometimes difficult to find a plausible candidate for the referent. To what does 'pencil' refer? Not to any particular pencil, for the word 'pencil' can be used in talking about any pencil whatsoever. If saying what the word refers to is to bring out what gives it its semantic status, what enables it to function as it does, then we cannot limit its reference to any particular pencil or to any particular group of pencils. The most plausible suggestion would be that it refers to the class of pencils, that is, to the sum total of all those objects correctly called "pencils." Likewise, 'courageous' might be said to refer to a certain quality of character, the quality of courage. And 'run' could be said to refer to the class of all acts of running. It is to be noted that in order to find anything that might conceivably be a referent for words of these sorts (which make up the great bulk of our vocabulary), we have had to bring in entities of a rather abstract sort—classes and qualities. This should not disturb us, unless we are attached to the groundless idea that words cannot be meaningful unless they refer to concrete observable physical objects.

There is no doubt that 'pencil' is related in some important way to the class of pencils, but does it *refer* to that class? One reason for denying that it does is this. If we want to pick out the class of pencils as what we are talking about, preparatory to going on to say something about it, the word 'pencil' will not serve our purpose. If, for example, we want to say that the class of pencils is very large, we will not succeed in doing so by uttering the sentence "Pencil is very large." The word 'pencil' simply will not do the job of referring to the class of pencils. The same point can be made for adjectives and verbs. If we wanted to pick out the quality of courage in order to say something about it, for example, that it is all too rare in these times, we could not use the adjective 'courageous' to do so. We would not say "Courageous is all too rare in these times." Again, I would not say that what I just did belongs to the class of acts of running by uttering the sentence "What I just did belongs to run."

This point reflects the fact that referring is only one of the functions that linguistic expressions perform, a function assigned to some sorts of expressions and not to others. What distinguishes referring from other functions is the fact that it serves to make explicit what a given bit of discourse is about. Thus:

W refers to $x =_{df}$. W can be used in a sentence, S, to make it explicit that S is about x.

There are other contexts in which expressions are used to refer to something, for example, in lists, or in labels. But we may take the function of making explicit what a sentence is about as the defining characteristic of referring. Types of expressions that normally have this function include proper names like 'Winston Churchill'; abstract nouns like 'courage'; phrases combining a concrete noun or noun phrase with an article or demonstrative, like 'the pencil,' 'this pencil,' 'the pencil in my pocket'; and concrete nouns in the plural, like 'pencils,' and 'dogs.' If referring is one linguistic job among others and is assigned only to some types of expressions, no account of meaning that presupposes that all meaningful units refer to something can be correct. More specifically, it cannot be the case that to say a word has a certain meaning is to say it refers to something.

But perhaps it is just that 'refer' is an unfortunate term for what the referential theorist really has in mind. In the preceding discussion, we used the term 'stand for' at one place; and there are other terms that occur in expositions of this kind of theory, such as 'designate,' 'signify,' 'denote.' Perhaps there is some more generic notion, such as 'standing for,' which is such that every meaningful linguistic unit stands for something. Referring would then be only one species of this genus, along with denoting, connoting, and any others there may be.

**Denotation and connotation**   Is it the case that there is some one semantically important relation that each meaningful linguistic unit has to something or other? Now there is no doubt that expressions like 'pencil' and 'courageous,' which do not, in the strict sense, *refer* to anything, stand in relations that are crucial for their meaning. Thus, 'pencil,' though it does not *refer* to the class of pencils, does *denote* that class; which is simply to say that the class of pencils is the class of all those things to which the word 'pencil' can be correctly applied. And, clearly, it is crucial for its having the meaning it has that it denote this class rather than some other. If it denoted another class, for example, the class of chairs, it would not have the same meaning, and vice versa. Again, although the adjective 'courageous' does not *refer* to the disposition to remain steadfast in the face of danger, it does *connote* that disposition, in the logician's sense of 'connote'; which is to say that the possession of that disposition by someone is the necessary and sufficient condition of the term 'courageous' being correctly applied to that person. Thus, it would seem that many expressions that do not refer to anything, nevertheless, do denote and/or connote something. Let us pause for a moment to give explicit definitions of these terms as they are being used here.

W denotes the class, $C =_{df}$. C is the class of all those things of which W can truly be asserted.

W connotes the property, $P =_{df}$. The possession of $P$ by something is a necessary and sufficient condition of W being correctly asserted of it (that is, of its belonging to the denotation of W). [8]

However, it is not at all clear that every non-referring expression has a denotation and a connotation. Consider prepositions like 'into,' 'at,' and 'by.' There is no doubt that each has a meaning, in most cases a number of meanings. For example, one of the meanings of 'at' is *in the direction of*; however, 'at' can hardly be said to refer, denote, or connote. We can see that referring is out, by the same argument as that given previously; we cannot use 'at' to pick out what we are going to talk about in a given sentence. To see that denotation and connotation are out as well, recall that 'denote' and 'connote' are defined in terms of an expression being applied to or asserted of something; hence, we can speak of an expression denoting or connoting only where it makes sense to speak of it being applied to or asserted of something. If you try to assert 'at' of something, you draw a blank. Having said that it is at, you have said nothing. To make sense you must supplement this at least to the extent of saying, for example, that it was thrown *at the wall*. But then, what you have asserted of the thing in question is not 'at,' but rather 'thrown at the wall.' This *phrase* could be said to denote or connote, but not the preposition itself.

It may be that at this point we are once more being victimized by the poverty of the existing semantic terminology. It does seem plausible to suppose that there is some distinguishable aspect of the situation we are talking about when we utter sentences containing 'at,' to which the word 'at' is related in some way not wholly unlike the way nouns or adjectives are related to what they connote or denote. We might try to formulate this aspect as *direction toward something*. We might then try to introduce a term that would designate the relation a preposition would have to such aspects of talked-about situations. But even if this is possible for prepositions, it still seems that such parts of speech as conjunctions and modal auxiliaries like 'should,' 'would,' and 'might' will resist such treatment. It seems impossible to identify independently any aspect of talked-about situations to which 'and,' 'if,' or 'should' is related in a way that is anything at all like reference, denotation, or connotation. There are those who have been so hypnotized by the referential theory as to insist, contrary to appearances, that such expres-

---

[8] Note that this use of 'denotation' and 'connotation' (some logicians use 'extension' and 'intension' instead) is very different from the literary use, in which denotation is something like the standard meaning of a word, whereas connotation comprises the associations, which may well vary somewhat from person to person, to which this meaning gives rise.

sions do stand for something. It has been said that 'and' stands for a conjunctive function, 'or' stands for a disjunctive function, etc. But this view runs into the difficulty that there is no way of explaining what a "conjunctive function" is, except by saying, for example, that it is what we are asserting to hold between the fact that it is raining and the fact that the sun is shining when we say "It is raining and the sun is shining." And this means that we cannot identify a "conjunctive function" except by reference to the way we use 'and' and equivalent expressions. Thus, we have not really gotten at an independently specifiable referent for 'and' in the way we can for 'Winston Churchill.' There we can specify what it is this name stands for, namely, the prime minister of Great Britain during the latter part of World War II, without having to bring into the specification talk about the way the name is used. In other words, to say that 'and' stands for a "conjunctive function" is just to talk in a misleading way about the kind of function 'and' has in sentences. No real extralinguistic reference has been demonstrated. Thus, there seems to be no escape from the conclusion that such expressions as conjunctions stand in no semantically interesting relations to extralinguistic entities.

Over and above the point that not all meaningful expressions stand for something in any sense of that term, there is a question as to whether the various types of "standing for" we have been considering have anything important in common. Is there anything semantically interesting that is common to referring, denoting, and connoting? If there is not, then there is no one sense of 'stand for' in which all the expressions that have these various relations to the extralinguistic stand for something. And it seems that there is not. Of course we can say that what they all have in common is that they are all relationships that 1. hold between expressions and what the expressions are used to talk about, and 2. are crucial for the meaning of the expressions. (The second requirement is necessary because otherwise the fact that the word 'pencil' is very unlike the class of pencils would be a relation of the sort in question.) But by bringing in requirement 2 we are making the account viciously circular; since the generic notion of 'standing for' is brought in to give an account of the notion of meaning, we can hardly bring the notion of meaning into an explanation of it. And unless we do, it seems impossible to find anything significant that is in common to referring, denoting, and connoting. This leaves us with the conclusion that (even if we forget about such items as conjunctions) the principle, "To say that a word has a certain meaning is to say that it stands for something other than itself," is either straightforwardly false, or does not employ 'stands for' in any one sense. And this means that we have failed to make explicit any single sense of the term 'meaning' in which all words have meaning.

The upshot of this discussion is that we cannot give a generally adequate idea of what it is for a linguistic expression to have a certain meaning by explaining this in terms of referring, or in terms of any relation or set of relations like referring. The referential theory is based on an important insight—that language is used to talk about things outside (as well as inside) language, and that the suitability of an expression for such talk is somehow crucial for its having the meaning it has. But in the referential theory, this insight is ruined through over-simplification. The essential connection of language with "the world," with what is talked about, is represented as a piecemeal correlation of meaningful linguistic units with distinguishable components of the world. What the preceding discussion has shown is that the connection is not so simple as that. Speech does not consist of producing a sequence of labels, each of which is attached to something in "the world." Some of the meaningful components of the sentences we use to talk about the world can be connected in semantically important ways to distinguishable components of the world, but others cannot. Hence, we must look elsewhere for an account of what it is for an expression to have meaning, remembering that the account must be framed in such a way as to give due weight to the fact that language is somehow connected with the world.

**Meanings as a kind of entity**    If the referential theory of meaning is based on the fundamental insight that language is used to talk about things, the ideational and behavioral theories are based on an equally fundamental insight—that words have the meaning they do only because of what human beings do when they use language. These theories focus on aspects of what goes on in communication, in an effort to get at those features of the use of language that give linguistic units the meanings they have. These theories may or may not saddle themselves with the assumption we found to be fatally involved in the referential theory—that every meaningful linguistic unit stands for something, in some one sense of 'stands for.' When they do make this assumption, as is often the case, they bring in associations of ideas or stimulus-response connections as ways of explicating this relation of standing for. Thus, one may suppose a word stands for $x$ by virtue of being associated with an idea of $x$ (ideational theory), or by virtue of having the potentiality of giving rise to responses similar to those to which $x$ gives rise (behavioral theory). These theories, however, are not necessarily cast in this form; and since the assumption just mentioned has already been amply criticized in connection with the referential theory, I shall, in considering the ideational and behavioral theories, concentrate on problems that would be there even if this assumption were not made.

Before examining these theories it would be well to note a certain deficiency in the way the problem of meaning and theories of meaning are often stated. More often than not, when people set out to clarify the concept of meaning they do so by asking, "What sort of entity is a meaning and how does an entity of this sort have to be related to a linguistic expression in order to be the meaning of that expression?" Theories of meaning are quite often expressed as answers to this kind of question. Thus, the referential theory generally takes the form of an identification of the meaning of $E$ with that to which $E$ refers, or alternatively with the relation between $E$ and its referent; the ideational theory identifies the meaning of $E$ with the idea(s) that give rise to it and to which it gives rise; and behavioral theories typically identify the meaning of an expression with the situation in which it is uttered, with responses made to its utterance, or both. There is something fundamentally wrong with this way of conceiving the problem. This can be seen by noting that we run into absurdities as soon as we take seriously the idea of identifying a meaning with anything otherwise specified (that is, specified in terms that do not include 'meaning' or any of its synonyms or near synonyms). No matter what sort of entity we try to identify meanings with, we find many things that we would be prepared to say about an entity of that sort but would not be prepared to say about a meaning, and vice versa. Since many things are true of one but not true of the other, they cannot be identical. Suppose that, following out the behavioral theory, we attempt to identify the meaning of 'Look out!' with such activities as ducking, falling prone, and fending. That the meaning is not identical with such activities can be shown by the fact that although it is true that I sometimes engage in such activities, it can hardly be true that I sometimes engage in the meaning of 'Look out!' It makes no sense to talk of engaging in a meaning. Again it may be true that I have forgotten the meaning of 'Look out!' without its being true that I have forgotten the activities of ducking, falling prone, and fending. Such examples show that meanings and activities belong to radically different categories; something can be true of one without there even being any sense in the supposition that it is true of the other. This same point will hold of anything else with which we try to identify meanings. The cruder form of the referential theory (in which the meaning is said to be the referent) is most obviously in trouble in this respect, for anything whatsoever can be a referent; at least, we cannot mention anything that is not a referent, for we have referred to it in the act of mentioning it. This means that the identification of the meaning of an expression with its referent could be maintained only if anything could be true of a meaning that was true of anything whatever; a random sample of referents will suffice to show that this is not the case. For example, the phrase 'the father of pragmatism' refers to C. S. Pierce. If the meaning of that phrase were identical with its referent, we would have to be able to say, both intelligibly and truly, that the meaning of 'the father of pragmatism' was married twice and that the meaning often wrote reviews for the *Nation*. Meanings, however, do not get married and they do not write reviews. And so it goes.

The moral of all this is that it is a basic mistake to suppose that "meanings" are entities of a sort that are otherwise specifiable. If we are to speak of meanings as a class of entities at all, we shall have to recognize that they are so unique as not to admit of being characterized in any other terms. The almost universal tendency to raise the problem of meaning in this form may come from the supposition that in specifying the meaning of a word, what we are doing is identifying the entity that is so related to that word as to be its meaning. That is, it is very natural to regard:

1. The meaning of 'procrastinate' is *put things off*.

as having the same logical form as:

2. The capital of France is Paris.

and, consequently, to think that just as in 2 we are specifying the entity so related to France as to be its capital, so in 1 we are specifying the entity so related to 'procrastinate' as to be its meaning. The simplest way of seeing that this is not what we are doing is to note that, in general, what follows 'is' in statements like 1 is not a specification of any entity whatsoever. This is true of 1; 'put things off' is not a phrase that has the function of specifying a certain entity of which we might then go on to ask and answer certain questions. The generalization is much more obviously true of:

3. The meaning of 'if' is *provided that*.

Here it is perfectly clear that there is no such entity as 'provided that.' This is so, not because no such thing happens to exist, but because it makes no sense to suppose that it does, for the phrase 'provided that' simply does not have the function of designating some entity that may or may not exist.

Then what are we doing when we say what a word means? What we are doing is *exhibiting* another expression that we are claiming has at least approximately the same use as the one whose meaning we are specifying.[9] The primary reason for saying things like 1 and 3 is to

---

[9] For some qualifications to this conclusion see M. Scriven, "Definitions, Explanations, and Theories," *Minnesota Studies in the Philosophy of Science*, Vol. II (Minneapolis: University of Minnesota Press, 1958).

help someone learn how to use the expression whose meaning we are specifying; when we provide a specification of meaning, we seek to accomplish this end by telling the person that this expression is used in the same way as another one that, we suppose, the person already knows how to use. Thus, 1 is roughly equivalent to "Use 'procrastinate' in the way you are accustomed to use 'put things off,' and you will be all right." We will be misled by superficial grammatical similarities if we suppose that what we are really doing is picking out a particular example of a special kind of entity called "meanings." [10]

If this account of meaning-statements is accurate, the problem of meaning should be formulated as follows: "How must one expression be related to another in order that the one can be exhibited in a specification of the meaning of the other?" If we can agree to use the term 'have the same use' as a label for that relationship, whatever it may turn out to be in detail, then the crucial question can be stated: "What is it for two expressions to have the same use?" And since whenever $E_1$ can be exhibited in a specification of the meaning of $E_2$, $E_1$ and $E_2$ would be said to have at least approximately the same meaning, to be at least approximately synonymous, we can formulate what is essentially the same question by asking, "What is it for two expressions to be synonymous?"

This point concerning the right way to raise the problem of meaning has absolutely no implications as to what *kind* of theory is or is not adequate; any of the standard types of theory can be formulated as an answer to this question. Thus, the referential theory can be stated by saying that two expressions have the same use if and only if they refer to the same object (or perhaps refer to the same object in the same way). The ideational theory would be that two expressions have the same use if and only if they are associated with the same idea(s); and the behavioral theory would hold that two expressions have the same use if and only if they are involved in the same stimulus-response connections. Henceforth, I shall proceed as if the theories were in this form, even when they are not explicitly so put.

**The ideational theory** The classic statement of the ideational theory was given by the seventeenth century British philosopher, John Locke, in his *Essay Concerning Human Understanding*, section 1, Chapter 2, Book III. "The use, then, of words is to be sensible marks of ideas; and the ideas they stand for are their proper and immediate signification." This kind of theory is in the background whenever people think of language as a "means or instrument for the communication of thought,"

[10] For a more extended presentation of this point, see W. P. Alston, "The Quest for Meanings," *Mind*, Vol. LXXII (Jan. 1963).

or as a "physical and external representation of an internal state," or when people define a sentence as a "chain of words expressing a complete thought." The picture of communication involved is set forth with great clarity by Locke in the passage immediately preceding the sentence just quoted.

> Man, though he has great variety of thoughts, and such, from which others, as well as himself, might receive profit and delight; yet they are all within his own breast, invisible and hidden from others, nor can of themselves be made to appear. The comfort and advantage of society not being to be had without communication of thoughts, it was necessary that man should find out some external sensible signs, whereof those invisible ideas, which his thoughts are made up for, might be made known to others. . . . Thus we may conceive how words which were by nature so well adapted to that purpose, come to be made use of by men, as the signs of their ideas; not by any natural connexion that there is between particular articulate sounds and certain ideas, for then there would be but one language amongst all men; but by a voluntary imposition, whereby such a word is made arbitrarily the mark of such an idea.

According to this theory, what gives a linguistic expression a certain meaning is the fact that it is regularly used in communication as the "mark" of a certain idea; the ideas with which we do our thinking have an existence and a function that is independent of language. If each of us were content to keep all his thoughts to himself, language could have been dispensed with; it is only because we feel a need to convey our thoughts to each other that we have to make use of publicly observable indications of the purely private ideas that are coursing through our minds. A linguistic expression gets its meaning by being used as such an indication.

Let us see what would have to be the case for this theory to work. For each linguistic expression, or rather for each distinguishable sense of a linguistic expression, there would have to be an idea such that when any expression is used in that sense, it is used as an indication of the presence of that idea. This presumably means that whenever an expression is used in that sense, 1. the idea must be present in the mind of the speaker, and 2. the speaker must be producing the expression in order to get his audience to realize that the idea in question is in his mind at that time.[11] Finally, 3. insofar as communication is

[11] On a less stringent version of the theory, there can be occasions on which the expression is used in that sense without the idea being consciously in the mind of the speaker, provided that the speaker could call up the idea if any question arose as to what he had meant. These occasions would be those on which we are using words "automatically," "unthinkingly," without having our minds on what we are saying. But even this form of the theory maintains that the above conditions are satisfied whenever we say anything with our minds on what we are saying; and,

successful, the expression would have to call up the same idea in the mind of the hearer, with analogous qualifications as to an "unthinking" grasp of what was being said that might hold on some, though not on all, occasions.

These conditions are not in fact satisfied. Take a sentence at random, for example, "When in the course of human events, it becomes necessary for one people to . . . ," and utter it with your mind on what you are saying; then, ask yourself whether there was a distinguishable idea in your mind corresponding to each of the meaningful linguistic units of the sentence. Can you discern an idea of 'when,' 'in,' 'course,' 'becomes,' etc., swimming into your ken as each word is pronounced? In the unlikely event that you can, can you recognize the idea that accompanies 'when' as the same idea that puts in an appearance whenever you utter 'when' in that sense? Do you have a firm enough grip on the idea to call it up, or at least know what it would be like to call it up, without the word being present? In other words, is it something that is identifiable and producible apart from the word? Do you ever catch the idea of 'when' appearing when you utter other words—'until,' 'rheostat,' or 'epigraphy'?

What is disturbing about these questions is not that they have one answer rather than another, but that we do not know how to go about answering them. What are we supposed to look for by way of an idea of 'when'? How can we tell whether we have it in mind or not? Just what am I supposed to try for when I try to call it up out of context? The real difficulty is that we are unable to spot "ideas" as we would have to in order to test the ideational theory.

There is, to be sure, a sense of 'idea' in which it is not completely implausible to say that ideas are involved in any intelligible bit of speech. This is the sense 'idea' has in such expressions as "I get the idea," "I have no idea what you are saying," and "He isn't getting his ideas across." In that sense of the term, I don't understand what someone is saying unless I get the idea. But that is because the phrase 'get the idea' would have to be explained as equivalent to 'see what the speaker meant by his utterance' or 'know what the speaker is saying.' 'Idea' in this sense is derivative from such notions as 'meaning' and 'understanding,' and so can provide no basis for an explication of meaning. If we are to have an explication of meaning in terms of ideas, we must be using 'idea' so that the presence or absence of an idea is de-

---

furthermore, it maintains that this is the primary kind of situation, from which the automatic use of words is derivative. That is, a given person could not meaningfully use a given word without having the corresponding idea in his mind, unless he fairly often produced it with the conscious intention of making it known that a certain idea was consciously in his mind.

cidable independent of determining in what senses words are being used. Ideas would have to be introspectively discriminable items in consciousness. Locke was trying to satisfy this requirement when he took 'idea' to mean something like 'sensation or mental image.' But the more we push 'idea' in the direction of such identifiability, the clearer it becomes that words are not related to ideas in the way required by the theory.

The ideational theory will not work even for words that have an obvious connection with mental images, for example, 'dog,' 'stove,' and 'book.' A little introspection should be sufficient to convince the reader that insofar as his use of the word 'dog' is accompanied by mental imagery, it is by no means the case that the mental image is the same on each occasion the word is used in the same sense. At one time it may be the image of a collie, on another the image of a beagle, on one occasion the image of a dog sitting, on another the image of a dog standing, and so on. Of course a determined defender of the theory could claim that this fact is sufficient to show that the word is not being used in quite the same sense on these different occasions; however, if one takes this way out, he has simply lost contact with the concept of meaning he set out to explicate. For it is perfectly clear that such differences in mental imagery need not, and undoubtedly will not, be reflected in any difference in what one is saying. Conversely, one can have indistinguishable mental images accompanying different words with quite different meanings. Thus, the image of a sleeping beagle might accompany the utterance of the words 'beagle,' 'hound,' 'dog,' 'mammal,' 'animal,' 'organism,' 'sports,' 'hunting,' and so on. Clearly, this example does nothing to show that all these words were being used in the same sense.

**Meaning as a function of situation and response**   The behavioral theory of meaning also concentrates on what is involved in using language in communication, but it differs from the ideational theory in focusing on publicly observable aspects of the communication situation. There are several reasons for the attractiveness of such a project. One deficiency of the ideational theory that was not explicitly mentioned above stems from the fact that we do not look for ideas in the minds of speakers and listeners in order to settle questions about what a word means in the language or about the sense in which a speaker used a term on a given occasion. If I am not sure as to the exact sense in which you used the word 'normal' in something you just said, it would be absurd for me to try to find out by asking you to carefully introspect and tell me what imagery accompanied your utterance of the word. It is not at all clear just what we do look for in settling such questions; however, the fact that there is a broad consensus concerning what various words mean strongly suggests that meaning is a function of aspects of the communication situation that are open to public inspection. Moreover, the success of psychology in explaining some aspects of human behavior in terms of regular connections between observable stimuli and responses naturally gives rise to a hope of being able to give the same kind of treatment of verbal behavior.

The simplest forms of the behavioral theory are to be found in the writings of linguists who, not surprisingly, take over ideas from behaviorally minded psychologists with little awareness of the complexities involved. Thus, Leonard Bloomfield says that the ". . . meaning of a linguistic form . . ." is ". . . the situation in which the speaker utters it and the response which it calls forth in the hearer." [12] The crudity of this definition is mitigated by the qualifying statement: "We must discriminate between the non-distinctive features of the situation . . . and the distinctive, or linguistic meaning (the semantic features) which are common to all the situations that call forth the utterance of the linguistic form." [13] The requirements for the adequacy of this kind of theory are similar to those for the ideational theory. If it is to work, there must be features that are common and peculiar to all the situations in which a given expression is uttered in a given sense, and there must be features common and peculiar to all the responses that are made to the utterance of a given expression in a given sense. (Furthermore, these common elements must be actually employed as criteria for assigning the sense in question to that expression. But if the preceding requirements are not satisfied, we do not have to worry about this one.) Again, this seems not to be the case. Certainly, for a single word like 'shirt,' there is nothing of interest that is common and peculiar to the situations in which the following utterances are made or to the responses they call forth.

> Bring me my shirt.
> This shirt is frayed.
> I need a new shirt.
> Shirts were rarely worn before the fourteenth century.
> What a lovely shirt!
> Do you wear a size 15 shirt?

Perhaps we would do better to start with sentences, leaving subsentential units for later treatment. But even here the prospects are discouraging.

> 1. Bring me another cup of coffee, please.
> 2. My shirt is torn.

[12] *Language* (London: George Allen & Unwin, Ltd., 1935), p. 139.
[13] *Ibid.*, p. 141.

    3. What a superb steak!

If we abandon counsels of perfection and overlook a few exceptions, we can find situational features that are common to *most* of the occasions on which each of the preceding sentences are uttered. For example (using $S$ as an abbreviation for 'the speaker' and $H$ as an abbreviation for 'the hearer'):

    1. $S$ has recently had a cup of coffee.
       $H$ is in a position to bring $S$ a cup of coffee.
    2. $S$ possesses a shirt.
       $S$ is doing something to call $H$'s attention to one of his shirts.
    3. $S$ is doing something to call $H$'s attention to some particular steak.
       $S$ is enthusiastic about the steak.

Items like these, however, will not do the job, for several reasons.

    First, these uniformities hold equally for quite different sentences with quite different meanings. Thus, the situational features listed for sentence 1 hold just as often for the sentence 'No more coffee, please,' and the situational features for sentence 2 are equally correlated with the sentence 'Bring me my torn shirt.'

    Second, we have been considering the favorable cases. With declarative sentences that have to do with states of affairs remote from the situation of utterance, we are hard pressed to find any common situational features, at least any that seem likely to have an important bearing on the meaning of the sentence. Consider the sentences:

    4. The disarmament conference is about to collapse.
    5. Mozart wrote *Idomeneo* at the age of 25.
    6. Affirming the consequent produces a fallacious argument.

Each of these sentences can be uttered in a wide variety of situations, and there is little or nothing of relevance that they have in common. There are certain temporal limitations for 4 and 5. Thus, 4 is usually uttered while a disarmament conference is going on, and 5 is uttered only after 1781. But it is obvious that these uniformities are radically insufficient to distinguish these sentences from many others with quite different meanings.

    Third, in all these cases we are going to have great difficulty in finding any interesting features common to the overt responses made to the utterance of the sentences. Imperatives look most promising in this respect, for they clearly call for a specific response from the hearer. But in what proportion of the cases in which an imperative is heard and understood is the standard compliance forthcoming? Think of the variety of responses that a parent's "Come in now" will elicit.

    No response. Whatever activity was in progress proceeds as if the utterance had not been made.

Explicit refusal to comply.
Demand for justification.
Criticism of the parent for issuing the command.
Justification of noncompliance.
Plea for mercy.
Change of subject.
Running in the opposite direction.
Compliance.

If the response last mentioned were made in a substantial proportion of cases, the life of a parent would be much easier. And imperatives constitute the favorable case. With assertions, it is much more difficult to suggest even a plausible candidate for a common response.

**Meaning as a function of behavioral dispositions**    Psychologists and psychologically oriented philosophers who have taken this kind of approach to meaning have tried to develop more sophisticated accounts. Interestingly enough, they have pretty much confined themselves to responses to linguistic utterances and have said little about the situation of utterance as a determinant of meaning. Presumably this is so because they have generally started with natural signs, where there is no intentional production of the sign. In concentrating on responses, men like the philosopher, Charles Morris, and the psychologist, Charles Osgood,[14] recognize that having a certain meaning cannot be simply identified with regularly evoking a certain overt response, for, as noted previously, *a.* we can have meaningful utterances that evoke no response at all, and *b.* where there are overt responses, they can vary widely among themselves without any variation in meaning. Something more elaborate is called for. This, Morris tries to provide in the concept of a disposition to respond.[15] To say that someone has a disposition to make a certain response, R, is simply to say that there are conditions, C, under which he will do R. It is to assert a certain hypothetical proposition of him— 'if C, then R.' Now, even though there is no one response that is universally, or even generally, elicited by the utterance of "Come in now," it may be that this utterance regularly produces a *disposition* to come in if the hearer has a strong inclination to obey the speaker. In other words, it may be that this utterance brings it about that a certain hypothetical proposition comes to be true, namely, that if the hearer is generally inclined to obey the speaker, he will come into the house. This is what Morris is banking on. If this is generally the case, then

---

[14] See his *Method and Theory in Experimental Psychology* (New York: Oxford University Press, 1953), Chap. 16.
[15] See his *Signs, Language, and Behavior* (Englewood Cliffs, N. J.: Prentice-Hall, Inc., 1946), especially Chap. 1.

we can specify something of a behavioral character that is common to all utterances of a given sentence even though there be nothing overt that is common.

Unfortunately, this version of the behavioral theory fares almost as badly as the simpler one. There are several reasons why it breaks down.

1. If we try to specify the particular disposition(s), the regular production of which would give a particular sentence the meaning it has, we can think of some plausible candidates for certain kinds of sentences, for example, imperatives like "Come in now," and declarative sentences that have to do with matters of fact that have a direct bearing on the hearer's future conduct. As an example of the latter, consider 'Your son is ill.' We might think of this sentence as regularly producing a disposition to go where the hearer believes his son to be if he has a great deal of concern for him. But when we consider utterances having to do with matters more remote from practical concerns of the moment, things do not go so well. What semantically important dispositions are produced by historical utterances like 'Mozart wrote *Idomeneo* at the age of 25'? It may be said that this produces a disposition to say '25' if one is asked "At what age did Mozart write *Idomeneo?*" But if this is the only kind of disposition we can specify, we are in trouble. For presumably the meaning of a sentence has something to do with its connection with the sorts of things it is used to talk about; consequently, the meaning of a sentence that is not about language can hardly be a function of purely linguistic dispositions.

2. In fact, it is only in one sort of case that an utterance like 'Your son is ill' will produce a disposition to go to where one believes one's son to be if one has a great deal of concern for one's son. This kind of case is one in which the hearer believes that the speaker is providing correct information and the hearer has not previously acquired that information. If I do not believe you when you say "Your son is ill," your utterance will certainly not produce any such disposition. And if I were already aware of the fact, no such disposition will be produced by your utterance. I will already have been so disposed if I am going to be.

3. Even in the ideal case there are problems. For one thing, we may have to make a given disposition extremely, perhaps indefinitely, complicated before there is any plausibility in supposing that it is regularly produced by the utterance of a certain sentence. Thus, even if I understand and believe someone when he tells me that my son is ill, and even if I were not previously aware of this, this utterance will not lead me to go to him, even given concern on my part, if I am in jail and cannot escape, or if I am at the crucial stage of some enormous business transaction that will affect my financial situation for years (and

I have not been told that he is *seriously* ill), or if I have very strong religious scruples against travelling on a certain day, and so on. With a little ingenuity, we could keep going indefinitely in listing factors that, if present, would prevent the antecedent from giving rise to the consequent. Of course, for each of these possible interferences we could save the claim that the utterance generally produces the disposition in question by stipulating the absence of this interfering factor in the antecedent. Thus, the utterance of 'Your son is ill' will produce in a hearer a disposition to go to his son if he has a great deal of concern for him, if he is not physically prevented from doing so, if he has no religious scruples against doing what is necessary for accomplishing this, . . . However, it is not at all clear that we can ever complete this list.

Thus far in my discussion of Morris, I have ignored the fact that he has saddled himself with the assumption that every meaningful expression is a "sign" of something. Despite the indefensibility of this assumption, we can see why a behavioral response theory needs it. For if we were to allow *any* disposition produced to have a bearing on the meaning of the sentence, we would be dragging in things that have nothing to do with meaning. Suppose that uttering 'The sun is 97,-000,000 miles from the earth' produces a disposition to open one's mouth in amazement if one were previously unaware of this. It is obvious that this disposition-production has nothing to do with the meaning of the sentence. We can imagine a lot of other sentences with widely different meanings having the same effect, for example, 'The pyramids are several thousand years old.' With the assumption that every expression is a "sign" of something, we can limit the relevant dispositions to those that are dispositions to the kinds of responses that are involved in some important way with the object. No doubt it is extremely difficult to see just what such responses would be in the case of "objects" like the distance of the sun from the earth and the age of the pyramids. In fact, the difficulty of deciding which "responses" are to be called relevant to a given "object" constitutes one of the main weaknesses in Morris' theory.

**Summary of discussion of behavioral theory**   Whether we consider relatively crude versions that regard meaning as a function of common features of situations in which expressions are uttered and responses made to those utterances, or relatively sophisticated versions in terms of dispositions to response produced by utterances, we will be unable to find situation and response features that are distributed in the way the theory requires. Meaning simply does not vary directly with the kinds of factors highlighted in these theories.

Like the others, the behavioral theory is based on an insight that it perverts through oversimplification. Just as the meaningful use of language has something to do with reference to the "world," and just as in some way we do express and communicate our thoughts in using language, so it is also a significant fact that units of language get their meaning through being *used* by people, through the fact that they are involved in various sorts of behavior. Behavioral theories err in conceiving this behavioral involvement in oversimplified terms. They suppose that a word or sentence has a certain meaning by virtue of being involved, as response and/or stimulus, in stimulus-response connections that are basically similar, except for complexity, to a simple reflex like the knee jerk. Unfortunately, no such connections have ever been found, except for those that are obviously not determinative of meaning, like the fact that a sudden loud utterance of "Look out!" typically elicits a start. Some more adequate characterization of linguistic behavior is called for, one that will get at the units of behavior that are crucial for the meaning. We shall take up the search for such units in the next chapter.

# MEANING

# AND THE USE OF LANGUAGE

2

**Meaning as**
**a function**
**of use** It is a striking fact that in "behavioral" theories of meaning almost
no attention is given to what speakers are doing when they use
language. As I pointed out in the discussion of this kind of theory
in Chapter 1, many behavioral theorists try to construe meaning
solely in terms of the hearer's response. Even when something on the
speaker's side is brought in, as with Bloomfield, it is something about
the situation in which the speaker operates rather than anything about
what the speaker is doing in that situation. What makes this choice of
focus surprising is the fact that although the hearer may or may not
respond to what is being said, it will always be true that the speaker is
doing something (otherwise there is no linguistic transaction to consider). If we are proceeding on the assumption that the meaning of an
expression is somehow a function of what members of the linguistic
community *do* with the expression, the activity of the speaker would
seem to be a more promising place to look. Perhaps theorists have been
discouraged from taking this tack because they have supposed that all
we could say about the speaker's activity is that it consists of the production of a certain sentence. And because whatever gives that sentence
the meaning it has will have to be something beyond the bare fact
of its production (otherwise it would be impossible to have the same
sentence used in different senses on different occasions), it might seem
that in canvassing the speaker's activity we have only presented the
*problem* of meaning without doing anything to contribute to its solu-
tion. But as we shall see, it would be a great mistake to suppose that
this is all that can be said about the speaker's activity. Let us explore
the possibility of exhibiting the meaning of a linguistic expression as a

function of the way in which it is used by speakers of the language.[1]

This enterprise will have a chance of getting off the ground only if we start with sentences. For a sentence is the smallest linguistic unit that can be used to perform a complete action that is distinctively linguistic.[2] (If our concepts of linguistic behavior were more highly developed, we could define a sentence in this way.) Of course our ultimate interest is in elucidating the notion of the meaning of a word, for talk about the meaning of words is much more common, and much more important, than talk about the meaning of sentences. This is so because the primary use of specifications of meaning is in helping someone acquire or extend his mastery of a language. Specifications of meaning cannot be the only means employed, for before we can use them for this purpose, our pupil must already know enough of the language to be able to understand the specifications. By the time he has come this far, it is obvious that the most economical way of proceeding is to give him the meaning of individual words, and to let him use his already acquired practical mastery of sentence structure to put these words together with others in various sentences, rather than to tell him the meaning of sentences one by one. In fact, strictly speaking, the latter is impossible, because no limit can be put on the number of sentences in a language (for example, compound sentences can be made longer and longer without ever reaching a definite stopping place), whereas there is a finite number of words in a language. But if we are to see how the semantic status of an expression is a function of what speakers do with it, we must begin with expressions that can themselves be used to perform complete actions, and then try to specify component parts of these actions that are performed by component parts of the complete sentence.

[1] The idea that meaning is a function of use was forcefully stated in Ludwig Wittgenstein's *Philosophical Investigations*, tr. G.E.M. Anscombe (Oxford: B. Blackwell, 1953). Although many philosophers influenced by Wittgenstein have made use of this idea in discussing the meaning of particular expressions, virtually nothing has been done by way of going beyond Wittgenstein's cryptic remarks to an explicit analysis of semantic concepts. The theory briefly presented in this chapter represents pioneer work.

[2] This thesis needs qualification. For one thing, there are so-called one-word sentences like 'Fire!' But an adequate linguistic analysis would distinguish the word 'fire' from the one-word sentence 'Fire!', and would thereby relieve us of the embarrassment of having to recognize that the word 'fire' can be used by itself to report a fire. For another thing, any word can be used alone to answer a question. I can use the single word 'salt' all by itself to answer the question, "What's that on the table?" In this case, it is plausible to say that the preceding context permits 'salt' to function as an elliptical substitute for the sentence "That is salt on the table." Without a special linguistic context the single word 'salt' could not be so used. We can, therefore, state the above thesis more adequately by saying: "To perform a complete linguistic action we must utter a sentence or some expression which in that context is elliptical for a sentence."

At this point, let us recall our previous conclusion that what we are doing when we say what an expression, $E_1$, means is to exhibit another expression, $E_2$, which, we claim, is used in the same way as $E_1$. We can embody this conclusion in a definition as follows:

1. $E_1$ means $E_2 = {}_{df.} E_1$ is used in the same way as $E_2$.[3]

This means that the fundamental question is: "What is it for two expressions to be used in the same way?" ("What is it for two expressions to have the same meaning?"). If we can answer that question, then we will be in a position to make explicit what we are saying when we say what an expression means. The answer (for sentences) suggested by the preceding considerations is that two sentences have the same meaning if they are used to do the same thing. But before we can take this suggestion seriously, we must make some restrictions on the class of "things done" that we will be considering. One thing a person does when he utters $S_1$ is to utter $S_1$. But this sort of action will always be different when two different sentences are uttered; this cannot be the kind of action such that if two sentences are used to perform the same action they have the same meaning. And if we go beyond the mere sentence utterance to things that one can do in or by uttering a sentence, the suggestion seems to work for some things but not for others. Thus, I might impress someone by uttering either 'I have just been to dinner at the White House' or 'Toynbee just asked me to write a preface to his latest book'; however, this fact does nothing to show that these two sentences have anything like the same meaning. On the other hand, the sameness of meaning of 'Quelle heure est-il?' and 'What time is it?' seems to be due to the fact that they can both be used to ask the same question.

**Types of linguistic action**  What we need is a classification of the different sorts of actions that involve the use of sentences. In general, when a person utters a sentence, we can distinguish three sorts of actions that he is performing. 1. He utters a certain sentence, for example, 'Would you please open the door?'. 2. He brings about one or more results of this utterance, for example, he gets the hearer to open the door, he

---

[3] All the definitions of this form are to be taken with the presupposition that the person to whom the specification of meaning is addressed already knows how to use $E_2$. Otherwise, we would not get an equivalence between '$E_1$ means $E_2$' and '$E_1$ is used in the same way as $E_2$.' For, in general, it is possible to tell someone that two expressions have the same use without telling him what either of them means. I, who know Japanese, could inform you that a certain expression in Japanese is used in the same way as another expression in Japanese; and if I realized that you were completely ignorant of Japanese, I would clearly not be telling you what either of these expressions means. But if we add the proviso that the addressee already knows how to use $E_2$ (and that the speaker realizes this), then we will get an equivalence. Under those conditions telling you that $E_1$ has the same use as $E_2$ is telling you what $E_1$ means.

irritates the hearer, he distracts someone who is reading. 3. He does something that falls between actions 1 and 2, for example, he asks someone to open the door. The reason for saying that 3 falls between 1 and 2 is this. Unlike 1, it is not simply the utterance of a certain sentence. No matter what sentence is specified (for example, 'Would you open that door?'), it is conceivable that one might utter that sentence without asking anyone to open any door; one might, for instance, be giving an example or testing his voice. Action 3 does not go beyond the utterance of a sentence by essentially involving a certain effect, as in the case of 2. There is no particular kind of effect that the utterance must have if the speaker is to be said to have asked someone to open a door. His utterance may have the effect of getting the hearer to open the door; it may arouse amusement, scorn, terror, or incredulity; or it may produce no effect at all. In all these cases, it could be true that the speaker asked someone to open the door. I am not saying that an action of this category normally has no effect. I am saying, rather, that the truth of the claim that an action of this sort has been performed does not depend on the production of any particular sort of effect. We shall return to the question of the way this kind of action goes beyond the mere utterance of a sentence.

Borrowing some terminology from John Austin,[4] I shall call actions of these three sorts 1. locutionary, 2. perlocutionary, and 3. illocutionary. The distinction between illocutionary and perlocutionary acts is of crucial importance for our purpose. We can find many verbs and verb phrases that stand for actions of one or another of these sorts.

| *Illocutionary* | *Perlocutionary* |
| --- | --- |
| report | bring x to learn that. . . . |
| announce | persuade |
| predict | deceive |
| admit | encourage |
| opine | irritate |
| ask | frighten |
| reprimand | amuse |
| request | get x to do. . . . |
| suggest | inspire |
| order | impress |
| propose | distract |
| express | get x to think about. . . . |
| congratulate | relieve tension |
| promise | embarrass |
| thank | attract attention |
| exhort | bore |

[4] See his *How to do Things with Words* (London: Oxford University Press, 1962), lecture viii, ff.

There are two main distinctions between the two categories. 1. As already noted, perlocutionary, but not illocutionary, acts essentially involve the production of some effect. To say that I distracted or embarrassed or persuaded someone is to say that what I did had a certain kind of effect on the individual. But I can be said to have reprimanded someone or to have made a certain announcement, prediction, or proposal no matter what effect I had on anyone, if, indeed, I had any effect at all. 2. An illocutionary act, unlike a perlocutionary act, requires a locutionary act as a base. I can bring you to learn that my battery is dead by maneuvering you into trying to start the car yourself, and I can get you to pass the salt by simply looking around for it. But there is no way in which I can *report* that my battery is dead or *request* that you pass the salt without uttering a sentence or using some equivalent conventional device, for example, waving a flag according to some prearranged signal. 3. Another noteworthy difference between the two categories is that an illocutionary act can be a means to a perlocutionary act, but not vice versa. I can request that you pass the salt in order to get you to pass the salt and/or in order to irritate, distract, or amuse you. But I could hardly amuse you in order to request that you pass the salt, or get you to know that my battery is dead in order to report that my battery is dead.

To return to the problem of sentence meaning, the first pair of sentences presented on page 34 showed that for two sentences to have the same meaning it is not sufficient that they be commonly used to perform the same perlocutionary act (have the same perlocutionary-act potential). The second pair of sentences suggested, to use the terminology just developed, that the fact that two sentences are commonly used to perform the same illocutionary act (have the same illocutionary-act potential) is sufficient to give them the same meaning. A wider survey will reinforce the impression that sameness of illocutionary-act potential is what constitutes sameness of meaning for sentences. 'Das is gut' and 'That's good' are both used to positively evaluate something. In the cases in which 'Can you reach the salt?' and 'Please pass the salt' mean the same, they are both used to make the same request. 'That's my paternal grandmother' and 'That's my father's mother' are both used to identify a person in the same way. And so on. Thus, we can provide the following elucidation for specifications of sentence meaning.

$S_1$ means $S_2 =_{df.} S_1$ and $S_2$ have the same illocutionary-act potential.

**Word**
**meaning**
How are we to extend this account to words and other subsentential units? (For the sake of brevity, we shall henceforth use 'word' to cover all meaningful components of sentences.) A single word is not itself used to perform an illocutionary act. But perhaps we can think of each word within a sentence making some distinctive con-

tribution to the illocutionary-act potential of the sentence, in such a way that the omission of the word or its replacement with a non-synonymous word would bring about a change in the potential of the sentence. Thus, if we change 'Please pass the salt' to 'Please pass the sugar' or to 'Please dissolve the salt,' we have not made the same request; and if we change the sentence to 'That's the salt,' we have not made any request at all. Likewise, if we change 'That's good' to 'That's unfortunate,' we have not made the same evaluation. Thus, it would seem plausible to think of two words as having the same meaning if and only if they make the same contribution to the illocutionary-act potentials of the sentences in which they occur; and whether or not they do can be tested by determining whether replacing one with the other would bring about any change in the illocutionary-act potentials of the sentences in which the replacements are carried out. For example, the synonymy of 'procrastinate' and 'put things off' would consist in the fact that they make the same contribution, which in turn would be evinced by the fact that 'You're always procrastinating' would normally be used to make just the same complaint as 'You're always putting things off'; 'I never procrastinate' would be used to make just the same claim as 'I never put things off'; 'Never procrastinate' and 'Never put things off' would be used to make just the same injunction; and so on. This suggests the following elucidation of word meaning.

> $W_1$ means $W_2$ $=$ $_{df}$. $W_1$ and $W_2$ can be substituted for each other in a wide range of sentences without altering the illocutionary act potentials of those sentences.

Thus far I have been greatly oversimplifying the situation by talking as if each expression has a single meaning. In general, this is not the case. 'Can you reach the salt?' sometimes means *please pass the salt*, sometimes *is your reach long enough to enable you to touch the salt?*, and sometimes *show me whether you can touch the salt*. 'Run' has a great many meanings—*move rapidly, flee, operate, extend, chase,* etc. When there is more than one distinguishable sense, as there usually is, the most fundamental statement of meaning is "A meaning of $E_1$ is $E_2$." In such cases, we are only speaking loosely when we speak of *the* meaning of $E_1$. We engage in such loose talk when there is one meaning that is much more prominent than any of the others; thus, we might say without qualification that 'ill' means *sick*, even though in some contexts it means *unfavorable*, as in 'bird of ill omen.' Or we might use the phrase 'the meaning' when the context makes it plain which of the meanings is in question. Specifications of *a* meaning of an expression would be elucidated according to this theory as follows:

> A meaning of $E_1$ is $E_2$ $=$ $_{df}$. Sometimes $E_1$ has the use that $E_2$ usually has.

It has to be "usually" rather than "sometimes" for $E_2$ because the point of the meaning specification is to make clear the sort of use $E_1$ is being said to have sometimes; to do this we need to find an expression that is clearly connected with this use. If $E_2$ only exceptionally had this use, its exhibition would not clearly identify it. Expanding this schema for sentences, we get:

> A meaning of $S_1$ is $S_2$ = $_{df}$. Sometimes $S_1$ is used to perform the illocutionary act(s) that $S_2$ is usually used to perform.

The expansion of the formula for words is:

> A meaning of $W_1$ is $W_2$ = $_{df}$. In most sentences in which $W_2$ occurs, $W_1$ can be substituted for it without changing the illocutionary-act potential of the sentence.

The requirement that we choose an $E_2$ that usually has the meaning we wish to specify for $E_1$ is reflected here in the specification of most of the sentences in which $W_2$ occurs. To say that $W_1$ sometimes (but not necessarily usually) has the use that $W_2$ usually has, is to say that $W_1$ can be substituted for $W_2$ in *most* sentences containing $W_2$, but not necessarily vice versa. Thus, it would be quite in order to say that one meaning of 'case' is *example*. For 'example' predominantly has the use in question. But it would not be illuminating to turn this around and say that one of the meanings of 'example' is *case*. For 'case' is too strongly associated with other senses, for example, *box*. (Of course, a given person's linguistic background might be such that this would be an effective way of telling him what 'example' means; but this would not be the standard way to proceed.)

It will undoubtedly not have escaped the reader's notice that there is an important difference between our treatments of sentence meaning and word meaning. With respect to words, we have thus far only given an account of what it is for two words to have the *same* use; we have not also provided a way of characterizing that use which a given pair of words have in common. Two words have the same use when they are intersubstitutable in a certain way; but this criterion of intersubstitutability does not itself provide us with any characterization of the use the words both have. With sentences, on the other hand, we have done both of these jobs. Two sentences have the same use to the extent that they have the same illocutionary-act potentials; in specifying the illocutionary acts in question, we have specified the use(s) that each of the sentences has. This can be done for each sentence without bringing in the claim that another sentence has the same use. The notion of sameness of use is sufficient, as we have seen, for the elucidation of specifications of meaning; that is, if we can say what the conditions are under which two expressions have the same use, then we will be in a position to make explicit what it is we are saying when we say what an expression means. But there are other contexts in which the concept of meaning occurs, for example, talk about an expression having a meaning (without specifying what its meaning is) and talk about learning what an expression means and knowing what an expression means. A complete account of meaning would involve an analysis of these notions as well. For such an analysis, the notion of sameness of use does not suffice. For an expression to have a meaning, it is by no means necessary that it have even approximately the same use as some other expression; there are many meaningful expressions for which no approximate synonym can be found, for example, 'is' and 'and.' By the same token, to learn or know what an expression means is not to learn or know that it has the same use as some other expression. Even for those expressions that have synonyms, one can know what the expression means without knowing that so-and-so is a synonym of it. (This reveals a gulf between knowing what an expression means and being able to say what an expression means, for the latter capacity requires the ability to specify a synonym.) Where we are able to characterize the use of an expression, as with sentences, we can provide further elucidations. Thus, a sentence has a meaning if and only if it has illocutionary-act potential; and to know what a sentence means is to know what its illocutionary-act potential is—in the practical, know-how sense of being prepared to use it to perform certain illocutionary acts and not others and of being able to recognize misuses—not necessarily in the theoretical sense of being able to say what its potential is. In order to do these jobs for words, we will have to develop some way of characterizing uses of words. It is to be hoped that progress will be made along this line in the near future.

**Analysis of illocutionary acts**    To the extent that this analysis is, or can be made to be, adequate, it has the great merit of showing just *how* the fact that a linguistic expression has the meaning it has is a function of what users of the language *do* with that expression. This result has been achieved by concentrating on the appropriate unit of linguistic behavior, the illocutionary act. If this is the line along which meaning should be analyzed, then the concept of an illocutionary act is the most fundamental concept in semantics and, hence, in the philosophy of language. Thus far we have taken this concept for granted, relying on the fact that we have a large battery of terms in common use that stand for actions of this sort. No doubt, for all practical purposes we are able to tell well enough when someone is making a certain prediction, a certain promise, or a certain suggestion; and we are able to tell when the same illocutionary act and when different illocutionary acts have been performed on two different occasions. As with anything else, there are different levels of generality at which an illocutionary act can be specified; what someone did on a given occasion could be reported as making a request: requesting someone to open a door, requesting someone to open that door, requesting Jones to open that door, etc. But given a particular level of generality, we can handle the concepts fairly well. However, we saw earlier that when decisions about meaning become of theoretical importance, our unformulated capacity to wield the concept of meaning often falters and explicit criteria are required. When the notion of an illocutionary act becomes fundamental to the concept of meaning, these difficult questions of meaning will be seen to turn on questions of the sameness and difference of illocutionary acts; and in some of these cases, we shall again need explicit criteria. In the Introduction to this book, we saw that philosophers find it hard to agree on whether 1. 'I know that $p$' means the same as 2. 'I believe that $p$, I have adequate grounds for this belief, and it is the case that $p$.' On the analysis of meaning I have presented, this issue rests upon the question of whether 1 and 2 have the same illocutionary-act potential. But this question will have no more obvious an answer than the original one. If I say "I know that $p$," and you say, "I believe that $p$, I have adequate grounds for this belief, and it is the case that $p$," are we or are we not performing the same illocutionary act? Our native ability to handle illocutionary-act terms does not suffice here. We need an explicit account of what it is to perform a given illocutionary act.

Let us tackle this problem by taking a particular illocutionary act, namely, requesting that someone open a door, and asking what is involved in performing this act besides uttering a certain sentence or sentence-surrogate. We have already seen that effects on the hearer are not essentially involved. Perhaps it has something to do with the situation in which the sentence is uttered. Indeed, there do seem to be certain conditions that are related in some important way to this sentence.

1. There is a particular door that is singled out by something in the context.
2. That door is not already open.
3. It is possible for $H$ (the hearer) to open that door.
4. $S$ (the speaker) has some interest in getting $H$ to open that door.

That these conditions are important can be seen from the fact that if any of them is not satisfied, something has gone wrong with the request. If 1 or 2 does not hold, there is nothing that anyone could do to comply with the request. If 3 does not hold, it would be pointless to make the request of that person. If 4 fails, we have an insincere request. It is clear, however, that these conditions are not, as they stand, necessary conditions of the performance of that act, as, for example, the fact that a certain door is not already open is a necessary condition of opening it. If the door is already open, it is logically impossible that I should open it now. But it is not logically impossible that I should *ask* you to open it. I might have been under the mistaken impression that the door was closed (it was closed the last time I looked). In such a case, you would not deny that I had made the request in question. You would not reply, "You're not asking me to do anything," but rather, "What a silly thing to ask me to do!" or "How can I? The door is already open." These replies clearly imply that I did make the request. In a similar manner, the other conditions can also be shown to be unnecessary for the performance of the illocutionary act. For example, an insincere request is still a request.

One thing that *is* incompatible with the supposition that S asked H to open the front door is for S to (sincerely) reply to H's retort, "But the front door is already open," with "What's that got to do with it?" That is, if he is making that request, then he will recognize that a complaint alleging the nonsatisfaction of one of our four conditions is a pertinent complaint. (That is not to say that he has to admit that it is a justified complaint. He may maintain that the condition in question is, in fact, satisfied. But in so arguing, he is tacitly admitting that the complaint is pertinent.) We can put this in a less backhanded way by saying that in making that request S takes responsibility for the satisfaction of our four conditions. This is something like the sense of 'responsibility' in which an administrator is responsible for the efficient functioning of the departments in his charge. Responsibility for *x* being the case is essentially connected with the possibility of being called to account if *x* is not the case, and such a possibility can be taken as an indication of responsibility.

**Rules of language** There is an alternative way of putting this point, which is of considerable interest in that it reveals important affinities between illocutionary acts and various forms of nonlinguistic activity, especially moves in games. If we set out to analyze the concept of a serve in tennis, the problems we encounter will be very similar to those we have just discussed. To serve is not just to make certain physical movements, even given certain external circumstances. (I can be standing at the baseline of a tennis court, swinging a racket so that it makes contact with a ball in such a way as to propel it into the diagonally opposite forecourt, without it being the case that I am serving. I may just be practicing.) Nor are any specific effects required. A shot can have widely varying effects—it can inspire one's opponent with fear, despair, exultation, contempt, or boredom; these variations, however, do not keep it from being true that one was serving in all these cases. Then what does change when, after a few practice shots, I call to my opponent, "All right, this is it," and then proceed to serve? The new element in the situation, I suggest, is my readiness to countenance certain sorts of complaints, for example, that I stepped on the baseline, hit the ball when my opponent was not ready, or was standing on the wrong side of the court. I actually serve when, in hitting the ball in a certain kind of environment, I take responsibility for the holding of certain conditions, for example, that neither foot touches the ground in front of the baseline before the racket touches the ball.

In games, when such complaints are made, the plaintiff is said to be charging the other player with a violation of the rules. And he can, if necessary, back up his charges by referring to a list of rules for the game. In this area, the practice of making and accepting complaints has been "formalized" by the explicit specification of a set of conditions for the satisfaction of which a player takes responsibility at a certain stage of the game, and for the nonsatisfaction of which he will be taken to task. Thus, one can reformulate the above point about serving in terms of rules. One is serving only if in hitting the ball he recognizes that certain rules apply to what he is doing. There is no reason why we should not use the same terminology for illocutionary acts. Our point about asking someone to open a door would then read as follows. In order that S can be said to have asked H to open a door, S must utter an appropriate sentence, s, and recognize that the following rules govern his utterance:

> s is not to be uttered in that sort of context unless the following conditions hold:
> 1. There is a particular door that is singled out by something in the context.
> 2. That door is not already open.
> 3. It is possible for H to open that door.
> 4. S has some interest in getting H to open that door.

If the definitions given earlier in this chapter are adequate, it is the rules which are constitutive of illocutionary acts that are crucial for meaning. For according to these definitions, meaning is a function of illocutionary-act potential.

A complete analysis of even the relatively simple illocutionary act of asking someone to open a door would be beyond the scope of this volume. But I have said enough to bring out at least one crucial point. What is required for a given illocutionary act, in addition to the utterance of an appropriate sentence, is not that certain environmental conditions actually hold or even that the speaker believe them to hold, but only that he take responsibility for their holding. In other words, what is required is that he recognize that what he is doing is governed by rules requiring that the conditions hold. Thus, the conditions are involved in the act in a rather subtle way, one that is easily missed. Having seen this point, we can use our sample act as a schema for the analysis of any illocutionary act. To get a list of conditions for which S takes responsibility in performing a given illocutionary act, the following rule of thumb can be employed. Ask yourself what conditions are such that if S were to admit overtly that one of these conditions did not hold, it would be impossible for him, at that time, to perform the act. (This is logical, not psychological, impossibility. That is, given this admission, one would not *say* that he was performing the act.) Thus, if someone says, "I know that that door is already open, but would you please open it?" and if he is using 'I know that that door is already open' in the usual way, he can't be asking you to open that door. He may be making a joke or testing your reactions to absurd utterances, but he is not asking you to open a door. If we apply this test to several different illocutionary acts, we come out with the following lists of conditions.

Advising H to take chemistry.
1. H is not now taking chemistry (or at least not taking a certain chemistry course singled out by something in the context).
2. It is possible for H to take chemistry.
3. S believes it would be good for H to take chemistry.

Telling H one's battery is dead.
1. S has a battery.
2. If S has more than one battery, something in the context singles out one of them.
3. This battery has lost its electric potential.

Expressing enthusiasm for Jones' plan.
1. Something in the context singles out a certain person named 'Jones.'
2. This person has put forward a plan.
3. S is enthusiastic about this plan.

Promising to read H's paper by tomorrow.
1. There is a certain paper of H's that is singled out by something in the context.
2. S has not yet read this paper.
3. It is possible for S to read this paper by tomorrow.
4. S intends to read this paper by tomorrow.

Putting the point in this way shows us how the rule-governed character of language is crucial for semantics. Linguistic activity is subject to more obvious sorts of rules, which are not so intimately related to meaning, and in some cases, not related at all. Linguistic behavior, like most other forms of behavior, is subject to moral rules and rules of etiquette. However, the fact that it would be impolite in certain circumstances to say "Your false teeth are loose" can play no part in determining the meaning of that sentence. (Many other sentences with very different meanings, for example, "The food is tasteless" would be impolite in just the same way.) Again, there are grammatical rules that govern the way words can be put together to form sentences. But although the fact that 'desk' can be inserted in the blank in the sentence, 'I've just bought a _____,' whereas 'if,' 'into,' 'scribble,' and 'lovely' cannot, tells us something about what 'desk' means, it does not tell us very much. It does not distinguish 'desk' from many other expressions with different meanings that could be put into that slot, for example, 'house,' 'dog,' and 'share.'

**Problems concerning synonymy**

To help give a more concrete idea of the theory of meaning here presented, I shall provide an indication, however sketchy, of the way in which it would be applied to a particular problem concerning meaning. For this purpose, I shall take the problem of synonymy.

It is often said that it is impossible to find a pair of words that are exact synonyms. This impossibility, or at least great difficulty, is reflected in the definitions given earlier in this chapter. According to my theory, two words are synonymous to the extent that they are intersubstitutable in sentences without altering the illocutionary-act potentials of the sentences. Perfectly synonymous words would be so intersubstitutable in every sentence. It was because of the difficulty of establishing complete synonymy that I defined '$W_1$ means $W_2$' so as to require only that $W_1$ and $W_2$ be intersubstitutable in most sentences without altering the illocutionary-act potential. Now I want to look more carefully at the factors that prevent complete synonymy.

The main reason why it is so difficult to find exact synonyms is that practically all words have more than one meaning. The more meanings a given word has, the more unlikely it is that another word will have exactly the same range of meanings over the same range of contexts. Thus, although 'sick' and 'ill' share the meaning *not well* in many contexts, each has other meanings that are not shared by the other. Thus, 'ill,' but not 'sick,' can mean *unfavorable,* as in 'bird of ill omen'; and 'sick,' but not 'ill,' can mean *tired,* as in 'I'm sick of doing that.' Insofar as restrictions on synonymy are due to a lack of coincidence of clearly demarcated senses, they are easy to understand.

But even if we restrict ourselves to those contexts within which a pair of terms seem to have exactly the same meaning, we are not at the end of our troubles! For even in such contexts, there are various differences that attach to the use of terms; and if these differences are differences in meaning, we may well be left with the uncomfortable conclusion that no two terms have exactly the same meaning in a given context. Let us survey some of these differences and then tackle the question as to which, if any, are to be called differences in meaning.

1. The social environment in which the utterance of a word is appropriate. We get something of this difference with 'sick' and 'ill,' the latter being more suited to polite discourse. A stronger contrast of this sort is found in 'sweat' and 'perspire.' Almost any two "synonyms" will exhibit this difference to some extent.

2. Associations. Any two words will show this sort of difference, but with many pairs it is not easy to give an adequate formulation. Consider 'earth' and 'ground.' 'Earth' conjures up all sorts of associations—earth mother, fertility, earthy qualities in people, the source of our being—that are lacking for 'ground.' Try rewriting Keats' lines, "Oh, for a draught of vintage that hath cool'd a long age in the deep-delved earth," as "Oh, for a drink of wine that has been reduced in temperature over a long period in ground with deep furrows in it." Such a paraphrase exhibits a number of differences in associations between near synonyms.

3. "Emotive force." We can find pairs of words that seem to be synonymous apart from the fact that one carries a certain attitude or evaluation while the other carries a different one, or none at all. Examples are 'stool pigeon' and 'informant for the police,' 'inexpensive' and 'cheap,' and 'office-seeker' and 'candidate for office.' We must distinguish cases where the attitudinal force seems to be the only possible difference in meaning from other cases in which this difference goes along with others. Good examples of the latter are to be found in the so-called "emotive conjugations" inaugurated by Bertrand Russell.

> I am firm, you are obstinate, he is pig-headed.
> I am righteously indignant, you are annoyed, he is making a fuss over nothing.
> I have reconsidered, you have changed your mind, he has gone back on his word.

It is clear that 'gone back on his word' simply does not mean the same as 'reconsidered,' quite apart from the attitude conveyed, and likewise with 'righteously indignant' and 'making a fuss about nothing.'

If differences like these are differences in meaning, then we do not have exact equivalence in meaning between any two words, even if we restrict ourselves to one sense for each word. (In fact, this conclusion would follow even if only 2 is a difference in meaning.) But are they differences in meaning? Plausible arguments can be marshalled on both sides. On the negative side, it can be pointed out that in telling someone what 'earth' means, we do not go into an account of the associations typically aroused by it; and in defining 'stool pigeon,' we do not go into the fact that to call someone a stool pigeon is to insult him. But against this view, it can be argued that the specifications of meaning that we give in everyday life, and even in dictionaries, are rather crude affairs and cannot safely be taken as a guide in theoretical matters. Moreover, if the concept of linguistic meaning is such that to know the meaning of a word is to be able to use it correctly, then a theoretically complete specification of meaning would have to include anything relevant for such guidance. And it would seem that if we do not realize that 'stool pigeon' is a term of abuse or that 'sweat' is a relatively vulgar term, we are not going to use it correctly.

On the account of meaning we have presented, these questions would be resolved by determining whether, for example, 'I'm sweating' has the same illocutionary-act potential as 'I'm perspiring,' whether 'it has been cooled in the deep-delved earth' has the same illocutionary-act potential as 'it has been reduced in temperature in ground with deep furrows in it,' and whether 'he is a stool pigeon' has the same potential as 'he is an informant for the police.' And given the account of illocutionary acts just presented, this would be determined in turn, by determining whether in uttering 'I'm sweating,' in normal circumstances, I would be taking responsibility for any conditions other than those for which I would be taking responsibility in uttering 'I'm perspiring,' or vice versa; and so for the other pairs of sentences.

Proceeding in this way, it seems clear to me that 2 does not involve a difference in meaning. I cannot see that in saying 'It came from the earth' I am taking responsibility for any conditions over and above those for which I am taking responsibility in saying 'It came out of the ground.' The fact that two words will normally call up different sorts of associations seems to be a fact over and above anything I am disposed to allow myself to be called to account for. It is not as if I will recognize the hearer's right to complain if 'earth' does not evoke rich poetic associations in his mind. With respect to 1, I am inclined to give the same verdict although this point is arguable. It is true that I may be taken to task for using the word 'sweat' at a ladies' tea, and I may recognize the justice of this. But this is not to say that the restriction of social context has any implications for what is being said; we have already noted that linguistic behavior, along with behavior of other sorts, is governed by rules that have no semantic importance. For a condition to be involved in the nature of an illocutionary act, it has to be such that if one were to overtly admit that the condition does not hold, he could not then be taken to be performing that illocutionary act. And it does not seem that one takes responsibility *in this way* for being in a certain kind of social context when one says "I'm sweating." That is, if one says "I know that I am at a D.A.R. tea, but still I'm sweating," he could be saying just the same thing by uttering 'I'm sweating' in this context as he would be saying by uttering that sentence on the squash court. The social context restriction affects not *what* is said but *how* it is said.

**Emotive meaning**  With respect to 3, we seem to be in a different case, although we must not forget to distinguish between expressing a certain attitude or feeling and evoking that attitude or feeling in the hearer. The mere fact that 'He's a stool pigeon,' unlike 'He's an informant for the police,' tends to elicit unfavorable attitudes toward the person to whom the term is being applied does not suffice to show any difference of meaning between the two. This is a difference in perlocutionary-act potential. But there is a difference in meaning if in saying 'He's a stool pigeon,' one is taking responsibility for having an unfavorable attitude toward him and is not taking any such responsibility in saying 'He's an informant for the police.' In other words, there is a difference in meaning if, having said 'He is a stool pigeon,' I am prepared to recognize that a response like "What's wrong with what he is doing?" is not out of order. And it does seem that there is such a difference in the cases cited. Thus, our theory leads us to recognize the legitimacy of the term 'emotive meaning' in some of its applications. We can distinguish between the "emotive meaning" and the "cognitive meaning" of a sentence insofar as we can distinguish, within the class of conditions for which a speaker would take responsibility in uttering the sentence, between those that have to do with the feelings and attitudes of the speaker and those that have to do with other things. Thus, we might list the following conditions for 'He's a stool pigeon.'

1. Some particular male person is singled out by the context.
2. This person is an informant for a police organization.
3. S has an unfavorable attitude toward this sort of activity.

We can say that 1 and 2 contribute to the "cognitive meaning" of the sentence and 3 to the "emotive meaning." But we would not be justified in speaking of the emotive meaning of 'communist' just on the grounds that it typically evokes unfavorable reactions, apart from any regular practice of using it in such a way as to take responsibility for the existence of unfavorable attitudes in the utterance of it.

It is worthy of note that by and large our approach preserves and provides justification for the common distinction between what is said, the way it is said, and the effects that saying it has, along with the parallel distinction between what is meant, the way of expressing what is meant, and the effects that this expression has. As these distinctions are ordinarily made, differences in social context would be said to belong to the second category, differences in association to the third, and differences in emotive force to the first and third. Everyone would agree that these distinctions will have to be made at some point; no one would suppose that the fact that someone spoke loudly, aggressively, or in a Brooklyn accent would have to do with *what* he said rather than with *how* he said it. And if my telling you that it is raining leads you to weep, it would be universally agreed that this is a fact about the effects of what I said rather than about what I said. One merit of the illocutionary-act account is that it justifies drawing these distinctions in just about the place they are ordinarily drawn.

**Problems about illocutionary acts**    The nature and variety of illocutionary acts is of interest for the philosophy of language not only because of their crucial place in the analysis of meaning, but for other reasons as well. In virtually every branch of philosophy, the analysis of one or another sort of illocutionary act sometimes takes over the center of the stage. In logic and epistemology, it often becomes important to get clear as to what it is to make a statement or assertion and as to the conditions under which we have the same statement or assertion made on two occasions. For example, much of the discussion of the nature of truth hangs on whether in saying 1. 'It's true that caviar is expensive,' I am making just the same statement (if I am making a statement at all) as in saying 2. 'Caviar is expensive.' The defenders of the correspondence theory of truth, according to which the truth of a statement consists in its correspondence with the facts, hold that in 1, we are not making a statement about caviar at all, but quite a different statement about the statement made in 2. Some of the critics of this theory maintain that in 1, we are not making a statement at all, but rather performing some other kind of illocutionary act, such as endorsing, conceding, or admitting what someone else has said. Other critics maintain that truth will lose its mysterious aura once we realize that sentence 1 is just a more emphatic way of making the very same statement that is made in 2.

The analysis of illocutionary acts also becomes of crucial importance in ethics. A great deal of ethical theory is concerned with getting clear as to what we are doing when we make moral judgments. We must be clear about this if we are to know what considerations are appropriate for supporting and criticizing such judgments. Actually 'moral judgment' is a blanket term, covering a loosely organized group of types of illocutionary acts—reprimands, behests, injunctions, exhortations, imputations of obligation, etc. The various positions in ethical theory can be most profitably distinguished by the different positions they take on the nature of such illocutionary acts. Thus, naturalists in ethics hold that in telling someone that he ought to do something, one is making a special kind of statement of empirical fact. Naturalists differ as to the content of the statement; one version is that such statements say something about the consequences of the action in question for human welfare. Emotivists, on the other hand, tend to assimilate imputations of obligation to expressions of feelings and attitudes. It seems that this problem could be discussed more effectively if an adequate method for analyzing illocutionary acts were available.

# LANGUAGE

# AND ITS NEAR RELATIONS

3

Thus far I have been taking the concept of language for granted. It is high time I undertook to give an explicit account of the nature of language and of what distinguishes it from more or less similar matters. This task is best approached by looking at the relation between linguistic elements on the one hand and various more or less similar items, such as signs, signals, diagrams, pictures, and religious symbols, on the other.

**The generic notion of a sign** Many theorists have supposed that items of all these sorts can be usefully grouped together under the heading of "signs." Words (and other linguistic units) would then be one sub class of this genus; language would be made up of one particular kind of sign. Thus, the following facts would all be regarded as cases of "sign-functioning."

1. Boulders of this sort are a sign of glacial activity.
2. A hum like that indicates a loose connection in the wiring.
3. That expression on his face means trouble.
4. That is a sample of forest green wall paint.
5. This is a diagram of an 80-watt power amplifier.
6. In early Christian art, a ship symbolized the church.
7. When the umpire moves his hands horizontally, palm down, that means safe.
8. A red light means stop.
9. Four bells indicate fire.
10. 'Plume' denotes pens.
11. 'Oculist' denotes eye doctors.
12. 'Equiangular' connotes the property of having all angles equal to each other.

13. 'Uncle Sam' is a nickname for the U.S.A.
14. 'Pinochle' is the name of a game.

Before we can accept the idea that words are to be regarded as one kind of "sign," it must be shown that all the facts on this list have something important in common. That is, it must be shown that there is some one sense of 'sign' that applies throughout the list. It is not obvious that there is. Note that as 'sign' is ordinarily used, it does not apply so widely. What would it mean to say " 'Plume' is a sign of pens" or "This diagram is a sign of an 80-watt amplifier"? (And the same is true of 'symbol,' 'signal,' or any other semiotic term, which one might try to apply generally to all items on the list. For example, a hum is not a symbol of a loose connection in the wiring, nor is 'oculist' a signal of eye doctors.) Thus, the general sign theorist must be using 'sign' in a technical sense and it is up to him to tell us what that is. Peirce's definition may be taken as typical. "A sign . . . is something that stands to somebody for something in some respect or capacity." [1] In this definition, the weight is being placed on the term 'stand for.' (Other definitions rest on similar terms like 'represent.') Is there any sense of 'stand for' in which in each case we have one thing standing for another?

Perhaps the most plausible move is to define 'stand for' as *call to mind*. Thus, the claim would be that what makes each entry on the list a case of sign-functioning is that, in each case, a part of what we are saying is that one thing calls the other to mind. (The rest of what we are saying would lie in what distinguishes one kind of sign from another.) But this suggestion will not survive scrutiny. It is clear that if boulders of a certain kind are a sign of glacial activity, they were a sign of glacial activity before anyone realized this. In fact, they would still *be* signs of glacial activity, even if no one should ever realize this. (This reasoning may be applied to cases 2 and 3 as well.) That means that the boulders would still *be* a sign of glacial activity even if they never called glacial activity to mind for anyone. When "general sign theorists" treat cases like 1 through 3 (signs in the ordinary sense of the term), in effect, they make use of the notion of x *being taken as a sign of* y, rather than the notion of x *being a sign of* y. *Calling to mind* may be essentially involved in the former notion, but these two notions are quite different. We have already shown that we can have the latter without the former. And superstitions show that we can have the former without the latter. Black cats are often taken as a sign of bad luck, but that does not show that they *are* a sign of bad luck.

[1] C. S. Peirce, *Collected Papers* (Cambridge, Mass.: Harvard University Press, 6 vols., 1931-35), Vol. II, paragraph 228. All future references to material in these volumes will be given by specifying the volume followed by a period, followed by the paragraph number, as: 2.228.

With respect to the other items on the list, *calling to mind* seems to be involved in some way. It seems clear that something could not be a diagram of an amplifier unless it sometimes led someone to think of an amplifier; and it seems that 'Uncle Sam' could not be a nickname of the U.S.A. unless it sometimes happened that a presentation of this name evoked a thought of the U.S.A. Even so, it does not seem to be the case that each of these "signs" calls to mind the appropriate object on each occasion on which it is performing its normal function. Is it always the case, when a ship is functioning as a symbol of the church, that seeing the ship in a painting brings the church before the mind? And is it always the case, when one understands an utterance involving the word 'oculist,' that the idea of oculist pops into one's consciousness as a result of hearing the word? The considerations we brought up in Chapter 1 in connection with the ideational theory of meaning are relevant here. As pointed out there, it seems impossible to verify the proposition that such ideational effects take place consistently. And insofar as they do not, it cannot be claimed that "sign-functioning," even for these kinds of items, *consists in x* calling *y* to mind.

Of course, one might modify the definition of '*x* stands for *y*' to read *x calls y to mind given certain appropriate conditions*. But the trouble with this suggestion is that any *x* will call any *y* to mind, given appropriate circumstances. In a way, this is all right. We would want to frame a general definition of 'sign' in such a way that anything could be a sign of anything else. But as terms like 'sign of,' 'symbol of,' 'means,' 'indicates,' and 'diagram of,' are actually used, their force is much stronger. To say that *x is* an indication of *y* is not just to say that one *could* condition a person so that presenting *x* to him would bring *y* before his consciousness. There is a distinction between *x* actually being an indication of *y*, and it merely being possible that *x* is an indication of *y*. It is no accident that these terms have this force. If it is true that we could set up an association between any *x* and any *y*, then to say that two things are so related that an association could be set up between them would be to say nothing about those terms. (That is, it is to say nothing, though it is to say something about the associative process.)

Finally, there is the point that *calling to mind* extends more widely than sign-functioning. Wherever there is any kind of ideational association, we have a person so conditioned that *x* calls *y* to mind. Thus, my childhood experiences might have been such that every time I see an apple tree, it brings to mind my grandparents' house in the country. But it does not seem that this kind of phenomenon has important affinities with the items on our list. Of course, having cut ourselves loose from any ordinary sense of 'sign,' we can, if we wish, count this as an example of "sign-functioning"; but if we do, one might well wonder whether the generic notion of 'sign' contains anything that is important for the kinds of cases we were originally trying to understand.

Other attempts to formulate a generic feature of "signs" are subject to similar criticisms. In Peirce's writing, and more explicitly in Morris', we find an account of 'stand for' in terms of 'taking account of,' where 'taking account of' is conceived in behavioral rather than ideational terms. That is, $x$ will be said to be a sign of $y$ for A to the extent that on being presented with $x$, A is led to take account of $y$. If we try to think this through, we will discover difficulties very similar to those we encountered in connection with behavioral theories of meaning. Such an account will not work even for natural signs of objects or events that have a bearing on our activity in the immediate future. One does not actually have to do anything to prepare for rain in order to take dark clouds as a sign of impending rain. When we go beyond signs, ordinarily so called, to other items on the list, it is even less plausible to suppose that any behavioral "taking account" of the object is always, or even typically, present. To recognize a diagram as a diagram of an 80-watt amplifier is not to do something that would constitute "taking account" of such an object. It is not as if one would naturally expect to find an 80-watt amplifier in the immediate vicinity. Still less does hearing the word 'oculist' typically lead one to get set for the aproach of an oculist (the announcing use of the word is not statistically predominant), nor does seeing a ship in an early Christian painting lead one to "take account" of the church (whatever that would be).

At this point, I propose that we abandon the attempt to provide a justification for our intuitive sense that all the facts on our list have something important in common. The review of possibilities we have just completed gives little ground for hope that we will ever be able to find a single sense of 'stand for' that is applicable to every case. If there is a point in classing them together, it is not because of any feature common to them all, but because of a "family resemblance" between them in respect to several different features, none of which is shared by all.[2] Whether or not there is anything to this notion, it will be in line with our ultimate goal of understanding the nature of language, and its similarities with and differences from closely related matters, to turn now to the task of bringing out the major differences between sub classes of our original list.

---

[2] For the notion of 'family resemblance' among the things to which a term is applied, see L. Wittgenstein, *Philosophical Investigations*, tr. G.E.M. Anscombe (Oxford: Basil Blackwell, 1953).

Given any list, there are various ways in which it can be sub-divided. With this one, we could, for example, discriminate between man-made signs, which would include 3 through 14, and those that exist apart from human contrivance, 1 and 2. Or we could distinguish between those that fit into an elaborate system of "signs," 10 through 14, and those that do not, 1 through 9. We will get the most penetrating first division by considering the kind of justification that would be given for each statement on our list. Without attempting a complete account of the justification in each case, we can note some important differences. Cases 1 through 3 and 7 through 14 are distinguished in the following way. A statement in the first group would be justified by claiming that, in fact, $x$ and $y$[3] are always or generally correlated in a certain way. Thus, 1 is justified by showing that, in fact, wherever one finds boulders like this, glacial activity has gone on in the past; 3 is justified by showing that, generally, when an expression like this has appeared on the face of this person, he has caused trouble in the near future. The correlation always involves a more or less definite spatio-temporal relationship between the $x$ and $y$, but this differs from case to case. In 1, it is spatial identity, with $y$ being before $x$. In 2, it is both spatial and temporal identity (insofar as hums can be precisely located spatially). In 3, $y$ is after $x$ in time, and they are spatially related not by being in the same spatial location but by being connected with the same organism. By contrast, a statement in the 7 through 14 group is justified by showing that there is something about the way in which the "sign" is used that makes it related to something else in the way specified. It is clear that there is nothing about a certain gesture, apart from rules governing the umpiring of baseball games, that makes it an indication that the runner is safe, any more than there is anything apart from the rules governing the English language that brings it about that 'oculist' denotes eye doctors.

Moreover, for each group, the kind of justification relevant for the other group is not involved. We have already seen that it is neither necessary nor sufficient for boulders of a certain sort being a sign of glacial activity that anyone respond to them, much less use them, in a certain way. It is equally true, although less obvious, that correlations are not essentially involved in the justification of 7 through 14. No doubt, there will often be some rough correlations for "signs" like these. Unless it were quite often true, in the community in question, that there was a fire when four bells were sounded, then that signal would no longer be used as an indication of fire. Again, if umpires did not by

---

[3] Using these variables for whatever fits into the appropriate slots in the schema of the form, '$x$ is a sign of $y$,' which we are taking as the *form* of all the statements on our list, despite the fact that we have been unable to find any sense of 'sign' in which all the statements on the list do assert that one thing is a sign of another.

and large use the signal specified when and only when a runner was safe, things would break down. But the relation is quite indirect. To say that the ringing of the bell or the gesture has the significance it has is not to say that such a correlation holds. One way to see this is to note that with cases 1 through 3, where a correlation is what is being asserted, if the correlation is not universal but only holds for the most part, we are to qualify the assertion of the sign-relation. Thus, if a certain expression on his face is only followed by trouble most of the time, we should not make the unqualified statement, 3, but a qualified one, such as "That expression on his face usually means trouble," or "That expression is a fairly reliable sign of trouble." However, the fact that sometimes the gesture specified in 7 is given when the runner did not touch the bag before being tagged with the ball by an opposing player (after all, umpires are fallible and perhaps even occasionally dishonest) is no ground for qualifying 7 by saying that this gesture sometimes (usually) means safe. And still less is the fact that 'oculist' is often uttered when there are no eye doctors around (or in any predictable spatio-temporal relation to the utterance) any reason for altering 11 to " 'Oculist' sometimes denotes eye doctors," or " 'Oculist' denotes eye doctors to a certain extent." That is, even though correlations with the "object" may be indirectly involved, they are not crucial for what is being said when we say what a linguistic expression or signal means, denotes, or indicates.

**Icon, Index and symbol**    Peirce has made popular a threefold distinction of "signs" into icon, index, and symbol [4]

Icon—a sign which refers to the Object that it denotes merely by virtue of characters of its own. . . . (2.247)
Index—a sign which refers to the Object that it denotes by virtue of being really affected by that Object. (2.248)
Symbol—a sign which is constituted a sign merely or mainly by the fact that it is used and understood as such. . . . (2.307)

This distinction, in terms of that in virtue of which the sign is a sign of something, is very similar to the distinction I have drawn in terms of the kind of justification that could be given for different statements on our list, except that in my version, one is not committed to to the assumption that there is some one sense of 'sign' in which, in all these cases, we have one thing functioning as a sign of another. It should be clear that the two classes we have so far demarcated are very close to Peirce's index and symbol. We have extended the notion of "being really affected by" to cover any sort of *de facto* correlation, but

[4] For a good discussion of Peirce's trichotomy see A. W. Burks, "Icon, Index, and Symbol," *Philosophy and Phenomenological Research*, Vol. IX, June, 1949.

otherwise there is little difference. Henceforth, I shall refer to "natural signs," as in cases 1 through 3, as indices, and items like 7 through 14 as symbols.

There are other interesting distinctions between indices and symbols, although they are often overstated. Thus, it would be a mistake to say that symbols are used in communication and indices are not. It is perfectly possible for indices to be used in communication, as when I bare my chest to show you that I have been shot, or as when a marooned sailor keeps a fire going in the hope that someone in a passing airplane or ship will see it and realize that someone is on the island. What is a decisive difference is that the status of indices, unlike that of symbols, does not depend on their being used in communication. This has the interesting implication that even when x is being used in communication as an index of y, an interpreter can correctly take it to be an index of y without realizing that it was produced or exhibited for purposes of communication. Thus, a passing aviator can quite reasonably and quite correctly take the column of smoke as an indication of human habitation without realizing, or even hypothesizing, that the smoke was produced in order to communicate that idea. Contrast this state of affairs with one in which the marooned sailor is sending up smoke signals according to some widely used code. In this case, the aviator could not take a certain pattern of smoke to mean *I have no food* without supposing that it was produced with an intent to communicate. Of course, he might notice that the smoke he took to be produced naturally exhibited that kind of pattern; just as people may find marks on stones, which are very much like Phoenician inscriptions, but which they take to be due to weathering. In such a case, however, the aviator would not regard the smoke as meaning, *I have no food*. Instead, he would say that the smoke looks like signals that have that meaning.[5] With respect to some indices, for example, yawns, the very reverse is true. If we believe that a given yawn was deliberately produced in order to make the spectators think that the person is sleepy, then we will not take it to be a reliable indication of sleepiness.

**The notion of convention**    It is commonly said that symbols (in Peirce's sense) are distinguished from other "signs" by the fact that their significance is *conventional*. I have largely avoided this term because it generally carries unjustified, and very probably untrue, assumptions about the origins of languages.

---

[5] This point is also brought out by the fact that before we can identify a given sound pattern as a word, for example, we must locate it in one or another language. The sound pattern 'link' constitutes one word in English, another in German. No such problem is involved in the identification of indices.

. . . After one person or group decided to use this to stand for that, other people decided to do the same thing, and the practice spread; that is, these symbols were adopted by common convention. . . .[6]

A symbol, such as a word, designates a referent by agreement or convention. Human decisions are thus required in order to establish the meaning of symbols and such decisions are arbitrary ones. . . . Names arise as a result of human agreements, or stipulations.[7]

I think these passages are typical of the less guarded remarks on this subject to be found in the literature. But on reflection, we can see that language, as such, could not have originated by having decisions adopted by "common convention." As Russell has said, "We can hardly suppose a parliament of hitherto speechless elders meeting together and agreeing to call a cow a cow and a wolf a wolf." [8] By the nature of the case, making agreements and conventions presupposes that people already have a language in which to carry on these activities. No one knows how language originated, but at least we can be certain that it was in no such way as this. However this does not show that the words in languages spoken today did not get their meanings by convention—for any such word acquired its meaning after a language was already being spoken in the community in question—but all the evidence is against it. We know very little about the mechanisms by which new words come into being and old words change their meaning, but what we do know about it indicates that conscious decision and deliberately adopted conventions have very little part to play. There are cases in which new senses of words are explicitly proposed, as when Peirce proposes to use 'icon' to mean *sign which refers to its object merely by virtue of characters of its own*. And there are cases in which a word, or a meaning of a word, is adopted by convention, as in the stabilization of scientific terminology by scientific congresses. But these are exceptional cases, pretty much confined to technical terminology. For the rest, semantic change seems to be largely an unconscious affair, a matter of habits getting established without anyone or any group trying to establish them.

Like the social contract theory in political science, the idea that words get their meaning by convention is a myth if taken literally. But like the social contract theory, it may be an embodiment, in mythical form, of important truths that could be stated in more sober terms. It is our position that this truth is best stated in terms of the notions of rules. That is, what really demarcates symbols is the fact that they

[6] J. Hospers, *An Introduction to Philosophical Analysis* (Englewood Cliffs, N. J.: Prentice-Hall, Inc., 1953), p. 2.

[7] L. Ruby, *Logic* (Philadelphia: J. B. Lippincott, 1950), p. 20.

[8] B. Russell, *The Analysis of Mind* (London: George Allen & Unwin, 1921), p. 190.

have what meaning they have by virtue of the fact that for each there are rules in force, in some community, that govern their use. It is the existence of such rules that is behind the fact that they are "used in a certain way," in the sense of this phrase that is relevant here. In Chapter 2, we made a sketchy beginning at indicating just how it is that the meaning of linguistic expressions is a function of the way certain kinds of rules govern their employment. Henceforth, we shall feel free to use the term 'conventional' purged of misleading associations, as shorthand for "on the basis of rules."

**Icons, pure and impure**

We have not yet identified Peirce's icons on our list. Can cases 4 through 6 be so identified? Before answering this question, we shall have to get clearer as to the nature of an icon. As we saw, Peirce defined an icon as a sign that signifies its object merely by virtue of its intrinsic characteristics, rather than by a causal or a "conventional" connection. It seems clear that $x$ can signify $y$ on the basis of its ($x$'s) characteristics only if it is similar to $y$ with respect to these characteristics. Hence, we can also define an icon as a sign that signifies an object by virtue of similarity to the object. It seems clear that similarity plays a crucial role in 4 through 6. A paint sample can play its role only if it is the same color as the paint of which it is a sample. The similarity involved in 5 and 6 is more abstract. In 5, it is a structural similarity between the spatial relations that hold between parts of the amplifier and the spatial relations that hold between corresponding elements of the diagram. That is, by looking at the relative position of two elements of the diagram, we can tell something about the relative position of the corresponding parts of the amplifier. In 6, a ship is fitted to be a symbol of the church because of a similarity in function. Just as a ship protects voyagers from the water and conveys them to their destination, so the church, it is believed, protects men from the snares of the world and conveys them to their ultimate destination. However, it is equally clear that conventions are involved in all these cases. This is most evident in 5, where we have to arbitrarily set up a correlation between elements of the diagram and elements of the amplifier before the structural similarity comes into play. This correlation can be established by having circles, for example, represent tubes and lines represent wires, etc., by verbally labelling various items on the diagram, or by a combination of these techniques. In 6, the ship is well suited to symbolize the church by reason of the similarity just mentioned; however, it is an artistic convention that the church is symbolized in this way rather than by other objects that would be equally well suited by reason of similarity, for example, a fortress. In 4, the main point is that there is a convention that selects from among the various characteristics of the sample those with respect to which it is functioning as a sample. No one expects the paint to have the same texture as the sample or to be of the same shape or weight. There is a convention operative according to which it is the color of the sample that is crucial. Thus, all of these cases are mixtures of icons and symbols.

The question arises as to whether there could be such a thing as a pure icon. It would seem that so long as we have pure similarity and nothing else involved, the "sign" would not have the typical use of icons, namely, that of helping someone acquire certain kinds of information about something. For if we just present someone with an object and leave it at that (perhaps making it clear that he is to take it as similar in some way to something), he has no way of knowing either to what he is to take it as similar or in what respects he is to take it as similar. It would seem that by any such procedure, we could not accomplish what is typically accomplished by diagrams, maps, samples, and photographs. The process is too uncontrolled. Of course, icons are not always used to convey information. Representation of the church as a ship in a painting does not have this purpose. But even here, we need a convention operative to make clear what the ship is intended to symbolize. We do get similarity operative all alone in the association of ideas; but as we saw earlier, it is doubtful that this should be counted as "sign-functioning" at all, even on the most liberal criteria. Perhaps the most plausible candidates for pure icons are to be found in primitive religious symbolism and in dream symbolism. In a primitive religion, ritual acts may focus around a bull, a mountain, or a sacred fire, without there being an explicit account of what gives these objects the significance they are felt to have. It might be suggested that what is happening here is that the bull, for example, is being treated as sacred because of certain characteristics it embodies to a marked degree, such as virility, even though none of the worshippers has formulated this as such. The bull could then be said to function as an icon of virility (or of other virile things), without this functioning being tied down by any conventions or rules. Again, in a dream, mountains may be functioning as a symbol of the dreamer's mother, solely on the basis of some similarity that the dreamer sees (without necessarily being aware that he sees it). But in areas such as these, it is notoriously difficult to get a clear idea of just what is going on.

**Language as a system of symbols**  It should be clear that language belongs somewhere within the category of symbols, in Peirce's sense of the term. Language is often defined as a system of symbols, and this can be accepted as a summary statement. However, it will have to be elaborated before it is very informative.

First, let us try to get a more concrete idea of the sense in which a system is involved. 1. The elements of language, such as words, are combinable in some ways and not in others; and the meaning of the combination is a determinate function of the meanings of the constituents and their mode of combination. (We can have 'Come in now' but not 'Now in come' or 'Come although now.') 2. Each constituent of a sentence can be replaced by certain words and not by others. This is partly just another way of saying what was said by 1. (Thus, 'in' in 'Come in now' can be replaced by 'over' or 'through,' but not by 'bookcase' or 'impossible.') 3. A new sentence can be constructed by transforming an old sentence in a certain kind of way, with a certain kind of alteration of meaning always attaching to a certain kind of transformation. Thus, the kind of transformation involved in going from 'Brooks resolved the problem' to the 'The problem was resolved by Brooks' carries with it a certain kind of meaning relation between the two.

The notion of language as a system of symbols will be misleading if we suppose that each of the symbols that enters into the system is what it is independent of its involvement in the system, so that it could be just the same symbol if it were in no system at all. A word is identified only through an analysis of the speech that is carried on in a certain community. We are so accustomed to the rather rudimentary analysis of our speech, which is involved in our writing system, that we are likely to think of it as an immediately obvious feature of the nature of things. In fact, the concept of a word represents a certain way of analyzing utterances into repeatable segments or segment-types; what is to count as two utterances of the same word, rather than utterances of two different words, is always more or less a question as to what decision will give us the most useful way of representing the language. Are 'is' and 'am' two words or two forms of the same word? How about 'wave' as a noun and 'wave' as a verb? Or 'ox' and 'oxen'? If we say that the first and third examples involve two different forms of the same word, while the second involves two different words, it is abundantly clear that the decision is not solely on similarity in sound pattern. This point can also be seen from the fact that in dealing with different dialects we will count 'aw' (Cockney) and 'high' ("standard" English) as the same word, even though the latter is much more similar in sound to the "different" word "nigh" than it is to the former. Thus, the elements making up the system that constitutes a language are not items that might have been what they are apart from any such system.

The above remarks bring out more than one way in which language is abstract. In this connection, we should keep in mind the often repeated, but seldom consistently observed, distinction between *lan-*

*guage* and *speech*. Speech comprises the totality of verbal behavior that goes on in a community; whereas language is the abstract system of identifiable elements and the rules of their combinations, which is exemplified in this behavior and which is discovered by an analysis of the behavior. Not only the system as a whole, but also each element thereof, is an abstraction from concrete behavior. (This is a consequence of the fact that the element cannot be identified apart from an analysis of the system.) We have just noted briefly the impossibility of identifying a word with a certain sensibly recognizable combination of sounds. A word is a certain disjunction of sound patterns, for example, 'aw' and 'high,' such that whenever one of these is exemplified (perhaps with further restrictions as to the linguistic environment in which the exemplification takes place), we will say that we have an example of that word. Thus, a word is more abstract than a melody, for example. It has the same degree of abstractness as a type of melody. It is still more impossible to identify a language with a series of events or aggregate of verbal behaviors. Every time I speak I add to the sum total of verbal behavior that has gone on in English speaking communities, but I do not thereby add to the English language. It is also noteworthy that the English language is something that might change over a period of time, whereas a sum total of acts of speech is not the kind of entity that can either change or remain unchanged; it is something to which new components may or may not be added.

# EMPIRICIST CRITERIA

# OF MEANINGFULNESS

4

It is an interesting and important fact about language that it is possible to construct expressions that at first glance look to be perfectly in order and yet are unintelligible. Uncontroversial examples of this phenomenon are such sentences as 'Saturday is in bed,' 'Quadruplicity drinks procrastination,' and 'My dream was three times as large as yours.' Although all of the words that make up these sentences are quite intelligible and although none of the sentences violate any commonly recognized rules of grammar (they are not at all like 'And the into when'), they do not make sense. We simply cannot understand what it would be for Saturday to be in bed (rather than somewhere else), or for two dreams to be comparable in respect of size. Now, if all the examples of grammatically impeccable but unintelligible sentences were so obvious, they would never have attracted the attention of philosophers, although they might have become of interest to linguists who were seeking to formulate the basic principles that govern the formation of intelligible sentences. It has seemed to many philosophers, however, that some of the sentences regularly employed by their colleagues suffer from the same defect, although less obviously. These sentences include the following:

1. The physical universe depends for its existence on an omnipotent spiritual being.

2. Properties have a mode of existence that is independent of their being exemplified.

3. A human being is made up of two substances—one material and one immaterial.

4. Physical objects are not just made up of properties; in addition, there is something (a "substratum") that *has* these properties.
5. It is possible that no human beings other than myself are really conscious; they may all be very intricate machines.
6. It is possible that the world came into existence five minutes ago, complete with records, memories, geological strata, etc., just as if it had existed for millions or billions of years.
7. Moral standards have an objective existence.

Each of these sentences plays an important role in one or another branch of philosophy—philosophy of religion (1), metaphysics (2 through 4), epistemology (investigations into the foundations of one or another sort of knowledge) (5 through 6), ethics (7).[1] Each of them has been put forward as though it were obviously intelligible, and experienced readers of philosophy have generally supposed that they understood what was being said when such sentences were employed. Yet the persistence of centuries-old disputes over such matters, the lack of any prospect of the issues ever being definitively settled, and the consequent doubt that parties to such disputes really understand each other have led some philosophers to question the meaningfulness of such sentences.

If one wishes to maintain that sentences that have been taken as meaningful for centuries are, in fact, meaningless, he will have to give arguments in support of his claim. And such arguments will have to proceed on the basis of some account of what is required for meaningfulness. Hence, the philosophers who have taken this line have felt the need to formulate criteria of meaningfulness. These criteria have generally laid down some kind of connection with sensory experience as a necessary condition of meaningfulness. In principle, we could have criteria that require quite different things, for example, coherence with other expressions in a system; but in fact, the formulations that have attracted attention have all been of an empiricist sort.

**Traditional form of an empiricist criterion**   We can begin by considering the kind of empiricist criterion developed by the British empiricists, Locke, Berkeley, and Hume. Without going into the details of the views of any one of these philosophers, we can present a composite view as follows. A word gets a meaning by becoming associated with a certain idea in such a way that the occurrence of the idea in the mind will set off (or tend to set off) the utterance of the word, and hearing the word will

---

[1] We could find examples from other fields, for example, psychology—"When a person is dreaming, he is carrying on trains of thought of which he is unconscious and which are hidden by the things of which he is conscious"; physics—"Everything in the universe is continually drifting further apart"; literary criticism—"A sense of

tend to bring about the appearance of the idea in the mind of the hearer. (See Chapter 1 for Locke's theory of meaning.) All ideas are copies or transmutations of copies of sense impressions. Therefore, a word can have a meaning only if an association has been set up between it and an idea that was derived from sense experience. In this way, all meaning is necessarily derived from sense experience. The British empiricists used this criterion to justify branding certain philosophical, theological, and scientific locutions as meaningless. Berkeley's celebrated rejection of material substance is a good example. Berkeley surveyed various terms that were used to explain what a material substance is, in distinction from its sensible properties, and how the substance is related to the properties. For example, it was said that the properties *inhere* in the substance, that the substance *stands under* or *supports* the properties. He then argued that insofar as these words are meaningful, that is, insofar as they can be given meaning in terms of sensory ideas, they designate sensible relations between things rather than anything that exists over and above sensible properties and relations. Thus, insofar as we use these words meaningfully, we are still within the circle of what can be perceived by sense and have not really succeeded in talking about something itself unperceivable, which stands in a certain relation to what can be perceived.[2] Hume extended this critique to all substance, mental as well as material, thus rejecting such terms as 'self,' as used by philosophers.

As the reference to Locke's theory of meaning indicates, this particular criterion of meaningfulness was tied closely to a certain theory of meaning. One would not put forward a criterion in the way these men did unless he accepted an ideational theory of meaning. But the real thrust of the criterion can be preserved when restated in terms of other theories. This thrust is constituted by the stipulation that sense experience play an essential role in the acquisition of meaning by a given expression. In terms of the behavioral theory, the requirement would be that the stimulus-response bonds, which are crucial for meaning, are acquired through repeated experience of the coincidence of such stimuli and such responses and/or other factors strengthening the bond. According to this view, the habit of uttering an expression in a certain kind of situation is acquired through repeatedly hearing the expression in that kind of situation, and also, perhaps, through having

---

reawakening powers and of limitless horizons was evident in Elizabethan drama." Sentences of these sorts, and many others, have been pronounced meaningless by philosophers. But for this discussion we shall concentrate on supposed examples of nonsense from philosophy itself.

[2] Actually, Berkeley later went beyond this restrictive view. See Book VII of his *Alciphron*.

one's utterance of the expression in that kind of situation regularly rewarded. On the referential theory, the requirement would be that an expression acquires the capacity to refer to a certain kind of thing through being paired with that thing in experience. It is this latter form of the empiricist criterion that rests on the notion of an "ostensive definition." To define a word ostensively is to get someone to realize what the word means by pointing to an example of that to which it refers (denotes, names, . . .), or to otherwise see to it that the person's attention is directed to such an object while the word is being uttered. In the immediately ensuing discussion, we shall concentrate on this version of the criterion, according to which ostensive definition is necessary for words to acquire meaning. We do this partly because it is this form of the theory that has had the most pervasive influence in our day (as in the "general semanticist's" view that we are not speaking intelligibly unless we are referring to something that can be "kicked"), and partly because it will enable us to avoid the extra complexities in which, as we saw in Chapter 1, the ideational theory entangles us. Instead of 'refer,' we shall use 'stand for' in a deliberately ambiguous way to cover any sort of semantically interesting relation in which expressions stand to what they are used to talk about. In this way, we can ensure that our discussion will have relevance to at least the great majority of meaningful expressions.

There are various reasons why an empiricist criterion has seemed to be acceptable, or even necessary. Perhaps the most powerful is this. Assuming that in some way meaningfulness depends on expressions being connected with aspects of the extralinguistic world about which they are used to talk, how is such connection possible? A given sound pattern is not related to one aspect of the world rather than another by virtue of its intrinsic characteristics; and we can hardly suppose that such linkages are innate to the human mind. (If they were, all men would speak the same language.) The only alternative seems to be that they are established by experience, through repeated pairings of the expression with what it stands for in the learner's experience.

Another argument is this. How could I have any reason to suppose that anyone else attaches the same meaning to a given expression that I do? Of course, we could each produce a verbal definition of the expression, but that will yield the desired conclusion only if we assume we are both using the words in the definition in the same way (and also that we understand the sentence form 'Give a definition of . . .' in the same way). And the question whether that assumption is true is a question of exactly the sort we set out to answer. It would seem that we can break out of this circle only if, at some points, we can test the hypothesis of common meaning without relying on community of meaning for other expressions. And how could we make such a test except by investigating the way the expression is or is not paired with experienced objects in the verbal activity of each of us? This means that such tests are possible only if it is necessary for meaningfulness (of at least some expressions) that such pairings exist.[3]

Empiricist criteria of the sort we are considering are usually stated as genetic theories about the way people learn what words mean or the way words acquire meaning. This is, in part, a reflection of the fact that in British empiricism of the seventeenth and eighteenth centuries, epistemology and semantics were not really separated from psychology. The separation is by no means complete today, but now we are well aware of the dangers of seeking answers to questions of fact, including psychological fact, by the traditional armchair methods of philosophy—reflection and clarification. If we really want to find out how people learn the meanings of words and what mechanisms are involved in such learning, there is no substitute for careful observation of the process itself; it is ill-advised to rest theories about this on *a priori* considerations, such as we have in the preceding arguments. Fortunately, it is not necessary to give these criteria a genetic form. In general, it is possible to replace any empiricist genetic account with a parallel statement of what must be the case for an expression to have a meaning for someone at a certain time—no matter how it acquired the meaning. Thus, in place of the Lockean genetic account, we can propose the following: in order for an expression to be meaningful in my current use of it, it is necessary that there be a tendency for the word to elicit in me a certain idea and vice versa. The formulation in terms of ostensive definition seems to be more wedded to the genetic form, but it can be restated without losing its empiricist force: a word can have a meaning for someone only if he is able to pick out its "referent" in his experience. This means that we have shifted from the genetic requirement that a word have acquired its meaning by way of an ostensive definition to the requirement that it be possible to give an ostensive definition. Since genetic formulations are thus easily convertible, I shall continue to make use of them for the sake of easy intelligibility. (The first argument just given for an empiricist criterion, which, as stated, supports a genetic criterion, could also be reformulated along similar lines.)

---

[3] Note that this argument is not available to "ideational" theorists like Locke and Hume, who hold that meaning is essentially a matter of intramental associations. For these philosophers, it is quite conceivable, though in fact not the case, that everyone should have a private language that he uses only in (silently) talking to himself, and that the words in such a language would have meaning in just the way words have meaning in the public languages that actually exist. Thus, for Locke and Hume, it would not be the case that the conditions of meanings being publicly shared are *ipso facto* conditions of words having meaning.

**The semantic**
**stratification**
**of language**

Complications begin to emerge when we note that it cannot be the case that every meaningful expression in the language gets its meaning through direct confrontation with an experienced referent. This account seems plausible for common nouns denoting observable physical objects—'tree,' 'house,' 'cloud'; adjectives connoting directly observable properties—'blue,' 'round,' 'shiny'; and verbs that are concerned with directly observable activities—'walk,' 'speak,' 'wave.' However, there are many other words belonging to these grammatical classes, whose meaningfulness would not be questioned by any but the most hardy empiricists and which could not possibly get hooked up with their extralinguistic objects in this way, because the kind of thing, property, or activity involved is not directly observable. I am thinking of such words as 'society,' 'conscientious,' 'intelligent,' 'neurosis,' 'language,' 'education,' 'brilliant,' 'manage,' 'pray,' 'prosper.' One cannot teach someone what the word 'prosper' means by pointing to someone prospering while uttering the word in the way one can teach someone what 'run' means by (repeatedly) pointing to someone running while uttering the word. Of course, one can observe instances in these cases. One can watch someone praying or (engaged in) managing a business, one can see a neurotic or an intelligent or a conscientious person and can even observe him doing something that displays his intelligence or conscientiousness or is a symptom of his neurosis. But the meanings of these words are such that it is not the directly observable features of such objects or occurrences that are crucial for the application of the terms in the way it is the directly observable features that are crucial for the application of terms like 'run' or 'shiny.' (One might cavil even at 'run,' if he thought that some intention on the part of the agent is necessarily involved in running.) To say that a person is conscientious is not to say that he exhibits certain directly observable features, which could be noted in a single observation; and to say that he is acting in a conscientious manner is not to say that his behavior exhibits certain directly observable features. One can't learn what 'conscientious' means by having conscientious people or conscientious behavior pointed out to one, because one could not see these people as conscientious unless one realized a lot of things about the people,[4] the realization of which requires having a great deal of language already under one's belt.

Thus, in all forms of empiricism except the crudest, language is divided up into semantic levels or strata. The fundamental level is made up of words that have their meaning by virtue of association with di-

---

[4] For example, that they had taken on certain obligations or duties, that they are now engaged in carrying out one or more of these, and that this present performance is only one manifestation of a fixed habit of promptly carrying out such tasks whenever they are committed to do so.

rectly experienced items; the principle then states that in order for other words to have meaning they must be definable in terms of words on this first level plus, perhaps, other words that have already been so defined. Some words get their meaning from experience more directly than others; but, directly or indirectly, experience is the source of meaning for all. This is the simplest version of an empiricist theory that is at all plausible.

It is a defect in such a theory that no one has ever made a plausible case for the possibility of defining all meaningful words in the language in terms of the lowest level. The most strenuous efforts have been made with theoretical terms in science; and even for such relatively low-level terms as 'electric charge,' 'specific gravity,' 'habit,' and 'intelligence,' empiricists have by now admitted that such definitions cannot be provided. Rather than go into the complexities of this issue, I shall focus on another difficulty that is both easier to exhibit in a short space and more revealing semantically. If, with Locke, we think of the basic level as containing word-sized units, then we are never going to get sentence-sized units into the language at all, which means that we are never going to be able to *say* anything; and in that case, there is no reason to say that we are dealing with a language. In order to understand and be able to use a sentence, one must not only know the meanings of nouns, verbs, and adjectives, one must also understand the significance of the syntactical form of the sentence; and for many sentences, one must understand various kinds of words that serve to connect nouns, adjectives, and verbs into sentences so as to affect the meaning of the sentence as a whole. One must be able to distinguish semantically between 'John hit Jim,' 'Jim hit John,' 'Did John hit Jim?' 'John, hit Jim! and 'John, please don't hit Jim.' This means that before one can engage in conversation one must be able to handle and understand such factors as word order; "auxiliaries" like 'do,' 'shall,' and 'is'; and connectives like 'is,' 'that,' and 'and.' These elements can neither get their meaning by association with distinguishable items in experience nor be defined in terms of items that can. Where could we look in our sense perception for the object of word-order patterns, pauses, or words like 'is' and 'that'? And as for defining these elements in terms of words like 'blue' and 'table,' the prospect has seemed so remote that no one has so much as attempted it.

**Logical atomism**   Thus, both from the analysis of what is involved in knowing a language and from a consideration of what seems to go on when one is learning a (first) language, it would appear that if we are to understand how language is based on experience, we must people our lowest level—where meaning is based on direct confrontation with experience—with sentence-sized units, not word-sized units. We have this form of the theory in Bertrand Russell's "Philosophy of Logical Atomism," [5] where the "logical atoms" are the sentences that could be used to report a single observation, for example, 'This is red' and 'This book is on top of the table.' We may call such sentences "observation sentences." (Russell wants to restrict the basic sentences to those that simply report the speaker's own sense experience, for example, 'I am aware of a round, bluish visual datum,' excluding those that make claims about publicly existing physical objects, for example, 'There is a blue saucer on the table.' But for our purposes, we shall restrict attention to sentences about physical objects.[6]) When the theory is stated in this way, we do not have the difficulties just considered. We have various sorts of syntactical structures, connectives, and auxiliaries built into the components of our empirical base, and we are not faced with the obviously impossible task of defining all such elements on the basis of (some) nouns, adjectives, and verbs.

**Verifiability theory of meaning**  When traditional empiricism develops into this form, it is very close to the kind of empiricist criterion that has been most prominent in the past few decades, the "Verifiability Theory of Meaning." This view was initially put forward by members of the "Vienna Circle," [7] a group of philosophers, mathematicians, and scientists that gathered around Moritz Schlick in Vienna in the 1920's. They, and those heavily influenced by them, are called "logical positivists." These men were concerned with the logic of mathematics and science and with giving philosophy a scientific orientation. They felt that philosophy in the past had been largely given over to useless controversy over metaphysical and normative problems that werc, in principle, insoluble.[8] Likc IIume, they felt that such controversies were fruitless because the participants were not making sense. It was in order to nail down this conclusion that they first introduced the principle that in order for one to be talking sense, he must be able to specify the way in which what he says can be empirically verified; in other words, it must be possible to specify what observations would count for or against its truth.[9]

---

[5] In *Logic and Knowledge*, ed. R. C. Marsh (London: George Allen and Unwin, 1956).

[6] This issue is discussed on p. 76.

[7] There were earlier foreshadowings, especially C. S. Peirce's "pragmatic theory of meaning."

[8] See the list at the beginning of this chapter for examples of propositions, controversy over which the positivists considered useless.

[9] Logic and mathematics were excluded from these strictures on the ground that they are made up of "analytic" propositions. In calling "$2 + 2 = 4$" an analytic proposition, one is saying that, like "All bachelors are unmarried," it is true just by

Let us not neglect the distinction between verif*iability* and verifi*cation*. In laying down verifiability as a condition of meaningfulness, the positivist is not saying that only sentences that have been verified are meaningful. Such a statement would be absurd; it would imply, for example, that we could not understand a statement until after we had established that it was true. The positivist recognizes that there are perfectly meaningful statements that have not yet been tested, and even meaningful statements that we are not now in a position to test. In requiring verif*iability*, the positivist is simply requiring that it be possible to specify what an empirical test *would* consist in; he is not requiring that the test have been carried out. V*erifiability is possibility of verification*. Furthermore, this does not have to be physical possibility or technological possibility. The positivist recognizes that there are perfectly meaningful statements that we are not, in fact, in any position to test. The standard example of this has been 'There are mountains on the other side of the moon,' but recent technological developments are forcing philosophers to change their examples. Perhaps 'There is life in other galaxies' will do for the foreseeable future. We have at least a rough idea of what sorts of observations would count for or against the truth of this statement, even though we are quite unable to get into position to make those observations. So long as we can give an intelligible specification of what observations would establish the truth or falsity of the statement, we have satisfied the criterion.

We should also note the specially wide sense in which the positivists use 'verifiability.' In this use, it is really equivalent to the disjunction 'verifiable or falsifiable,' that is, 'capable of being established as true or false.' Thus, the requirement is really that the sentence in question be capable of an empirical *test*. This is an important point, because the language used might give the impression that the positivist will recognize as meaningful only statements that can be shown to be *true*. (And how would we know in advance which these are?)

It may seem that the verifiability criterion is quite different from the ones so far considered in that it does not involve any stratification of language. Here, we apply the same test to any sentence; it is meaningful if and only if it is empirically testable. But as soon as we probe

---

virtue of the meanings of the terms in which it is formulated; hence, it should not be interpreted as making any claim to say something "about the world." Therefore, logic and mathematics were excused from the verifiability requirement. Although the status of logic and mathematics, and the concept of an analytic proposition, are highly controversial matters, we shall not have time to go into this aspect of the problem. In the ensuing discussion, we shall tacitly assume that these matters can be satisfactorily handled. For further discussion of this topic see Stephen C. Barker, *Philosophy of Mathematics*, in this series.

the notion of empirical testability, this can be seen to be an oversim-plification. Specifying an empirical test involves specifying a way in which a statement could be supported or attacked by the carrying out of certain observations. Thus, the statement 'Sam has measles' could be supported by observing that Sam has spots all over his body. This means that we must separate certain sentences in the language that could be used to report observations, "observation sentences" like 'Sam has spots all over his body,' which are meaningful just by the fact that they have this function. We then say that a sentence that is not an observation sentence, like 'Sam has measles,' is meaningful if we can specify certain observation sentences (not necessarily true ones and not necessarily ones that we know to be true or false) to which it is so related that each of those observation sentences could be used as positive or negative evidence. Once we put the matter in this way, we see that the verifi-ability criterion presupposes the same kind of stratification as the others. A basic level is singled out, the members of which have meaning in a specially direct way; other elements of the language have meaning only if they have the right kind of connection with the basic level. In fact, logical atomism and the verifiability theory are virtually the same theory stated in different ways. They sound different because the verifiability theory looks down from the nonobservation sentences, asking how they can be verified; while logical atomism looks up from the observation sentences, asking what else can be explained in their terms. It is, how-ever, the same topography whichever perspective we take.

The earliest forms of the verifiability criterion required complete verifiability. That is, a sentence could not be regarded as meaningful unless it were possible to specify a way in which it could be conclusively shown by empirical evidence to be true or false. It soon became obvious that this requirement was much too strong. It would exclude, for ex-ample, all unrestricted generalizations. If we take something so simple as "All lemons are yellow," it is clear that we cannot specify any finite set of observations that are such that having carried them out we can then be absolutely certain that this statement is true. Of course, a state-ment of this form could be conclusively falsified by a single observation (of a red lemon), assuming that there is no question of whether we do in fact have a lemon before us and that it is red. (These assumptions are together equivalent to the assumption that 'This lemon is red' is an observation sentence.) Just the opposite is true of the contradictory of this statement, namely, 'There is a lemon that is not yellow.' This statement can be verified by a single observation, but no matter how many yellow lemons we had observed we still would not have conclu-sively falsified 'There is a lemon that is not yellow.' Thus, we can find an unlimited number of simple generalizations for which we can specify no conclusive empirical proof, and an unlimited number for which we can specify no conclusive empirical disproof. This will be the case whenever we are dealing with "open-ended" classes like lemons, that is, classes that are so specified that no definite limit can be put on their membership, as contrasted with "closed" classes like the books in this room at this moment. Again, there are many apparently "singular" propositions that conceal unlimited generalizations of one sort or another, for example, 'Jones is conscientious.' To say of a particular person that he is conscientious is to say that he would react in a certain kind of way to a certain kind of situation, whenever or wherever it arose. (It might be more accurate to make this a statistical statement or a statement of tendency—that he would react in a certain way in most instances, or that he would always *tend* to so react in such situations. These versions would give rise to analogous problems, but in a more complicated way; hence, I will make the point with respect to the simpler interpretation.) It is to say that whenever he recognizes himself to have an obligation to perform a certain task, he does what he can to carry it out. But again, no matter in how many cases we have seen this to hold, we cannot be certain that the unrestricted generalization is true.

Thus, to require complete verifiability or falsifiability would be to throw out the baby with the bath water. Positivists soon came to modify the criterion so that it requires only the specification of observations that would count for or against the statement, which would serve to confirm or disconfirm it to a certain extent. "Confirmability criterion of meaningfulness" would be a more apt title for this revised version. Positivistically oriented critics of theology still take religious believers to task for not being able to say what observable happenings would count decisively for or against the existence of God; but in doing so, they are either lagging behind developments in the movement or unwarrantedly making more stringent demands on theology than on science.

The verifiability version of empiricism has suffered more than the others from a confusion between criterion of meaningfulness and theory of meaning. The common label, "Verifiability Theory of Meaning," would suggest that it is the latter that is being put forward and some of the more common formulations, for example, "The meaning of a proposition is the method of its verification," seem to bear this out. But a careful examination of the literature and a just appreciation of the predominantly polemic aims of the movement will show that what the positivists have really been concerned with is a criterion of meaningfulness. There has been little attempt to work out the notion that in specifying a method of verification for a sentence we are thereby giving its meaning. Such attempts as have been made are either unpromising or disastrous. A prime example of the latter is the suggestion that the meaning of an historical statement consists of certain investigations that we might carry out in the future in order to test it. That is, when we are talking about the past, we are really talking about the future! We will be quite in order if we concentrate on the "verifiability theory" as a *criterion* of meaningfulness.

**Deficiencies in usual formulations of verifiability criterion** As usually stated, the verifiability theory exhibits some glaring deficiencies that will have to be remedied before it can be taken seriously. First, note that it is not a *sentence* that can be said to be true or false (verified or falsified), but rather an *assertion* or *statement* that one makes by uttering the sentence. If we try to assign truth values to sentences, we run into hopeless dilemmas. Is the sentence 'I am hungry' true or false? On one occasion, a speaker might say something true. by uttering that sentence and on another occasion a speaker might say something false by uttering it. If we regarded the sentence as the bearer of truth value, we would have to think of it as constantly oscillating between truth and falsity, or even as being both true and false at the same time (if at the same time one speaker said truly that he was hungry and another speaker said falsely that he was hungry). But it *is* the sentence, not an assertion or statement made by uttering a sentence, that either has or does not have a meaning. Once we admit that a statement or assertion has been made, we have already granted meaningfulness. Meaning (in the sense in which we are concerned with it) is not something that a statement might or might not have. To avoid this difficulty, we shall have to revise the criterion as follows: a sentence has meaning only if it can be used to make an assertion, and it can be used to make an assertion only if it is possible to specify some way of verifying or falsifying the assertion. Stated this way, the criterion looks much closer to our analysis of meaning in terms of illocutionary-act potentials.

Second, even as so revised, this could not possibly be a general criterion of meaningfulness, not even for sentences. There are many sentences in the language that are obviously meaningful but that just as obviously are not usable for making assertions. These include, for example, interrogative sentences like 'Where is the butter?' imperative sentences like 'Please go out quietly,' and interjections like 'Splendid!' Such sentences are used to ask questions, make requests, or express feelings and attitudes. When we are using sentences in these ways, questions of truth and falsity do not arise; consequently criteria of meaningfulness in terms of verifiability have no application. It would seem that what we have is not really a criterion of *meaningfulness* at all, but rather a criterion of the usability of a sentence for performing a certain kind of illocutionary act.

Positivists have tried to take account of this point by construing their criterion as a criterion of a certain *kind* of meaningfulness, variously called "cognitive meaning," "factual meaning," and "literal meaning," which is then distinguished from something called "emotive meaning" or "expressive meaning." But apart from the absurdity of lumping the indefinitely various uses of sentences other than the assertive under the heading "emotive" or "expressive," one can question the significance of distinguishing different kinds of meaning in this way. If we are to say that an imperative sentence has a different kind of meaning from a declarative sentence on the ground that it is used for a different kind of illocutionary act, how far are we going to carry this? Are we going to say that 'Shut the door!' has a different kind of meaning from 'Please shut the door' on the grounds that one is used to issue an order and the other to make a request? And would we want to say that 'I was out late last night' has two different kinds of meaning on the grounds that it can be used to make an admission as well as to simply inform someone of a fact? If one is undeterred by this indefinite multiplication of "kinds of meaning," he may still well consider the fact that there is no reason to think that sentences of these different sorts have meaning, or get their meaning, in different *ways*. In each case, to have a certain meaning is to be usable for the performance of a certain illocutionary act; the differences simply come from the differences in the illocutionary acts involved. In each case, *what it is* to have a certain meaning(s) is the same. However, it does clearly make sense to speak of different kinds of meaning for sentences on the one hand and sentence-components like words on the other, for the account of what it is to have a certain meaning is different in the two cases. And still more can we distinguish the kind of meaning that a sentence and a knock in an engine have.

Whether or not one can properly speak of "cognitive meaning," the existing formulations of the impiricist meaning criteria are restricted to only one segment of language. This may not disturb those who are interested only in finding ways of ruling out supposed *assertions* that they find objectionable and in restricting scientific and philosophical discussion to questions that can be settled empirically. But to someone who is interested in the philosophy of language for its own sake, the restriction is disappointing. After all, it does seem that experience is and must be crucial for the way one attaches meanings to words, not just in making assertions, but in linguistic activity of all sorts; and it ought to be possible to find a criterion of meaningfulness that would adequately reflect this fact. The arbitrary character of the restriction can be brought out in this way. Let us take 1. 'The Holy Ghost descended upon us' as an example of a sentence to which a positivist would object as not being capable of being used to make an assertion that could be empirically tested. In this respect, he would contrast it with, for example, 2. 'John came down out of the tree.' Now it seems that any reason for regarding 1 as semantically defective would equally be a reason for regarding 3. 'Come, Holy Ghost, descend upon us' as semantically defective in contrast with 4. 'John, come down out of that tree.' Roughly speaking, if 1 is defective in contrast with 2, because we don't know what empirical observations would count as verifying it, by the same token, 3 should count as defective by contrast with 4 because we don't know what empirically observable states of affairs would count as compliance with the request. But as the verifiability criterion is usually stated, 1, 3, and 4 are all said to be lacking in "cognitive meaning," and as such, they are all lumped under the heading of "emotive meaning" or "expressive meaning." A theory that can make no finer distinctions than this is badly in need of supplementation.

Fortunately, the materials for such supplementation are ready at hand. According to the theory presented in Chapters 1 and 2, the meaning of a sentence is a function of its utterance's being governed by a rule that stipulates that that sentence is not to be uttered in a given kind of context unless certain conditions hold. This is a general account applying to sentences of all sorts that are used to perform illocutionary acts of all sorts. If this theory is acceptable, we have a way of generalizing the verifiability requirement so that it covers all sorts of speech. No matter what kind of illocutionary act a sentence is used to perform, the claim that a given condition required for the utterance of that sentence holds is an assertion that can be evaluated as true or false. Hence, we can give an unrestricted formulation of the verifiability criterion as follows: A sentence is meaningful only if its utterance is governed by at least one rule that requires that certain conditions hold such that for each of those conditions the claim that the condition holds is empirically confirmable or disconfirmable. Using this criterion, 3 would be ruled out in just the same way as 1 (if, indeed, either would be). For although 3 is not itself used to make an assertion that could be empirically confirmed or disconfirmed, its utterance is subject to a rule that requires the holding of such conditions as that there be some entity called the Holy Ghost, that it be possible for this entity to descend or enter into the human spirit, etc.; just the same difficulties that attach to specifying any empirical test for 1 attach to the task of specifying any way in which the claim that one of these conditions hold can be empirically tested.

**Problems
in the
formulation
of the
verifiability
criterion**

Now that we have the verifiability criterion in a more acceptable form, we can concentrate on some problems regarding its content.[10] First, there are controversies as to just what should count as an observation sentence. On the one hand, there are reasons for holding that no statement that makes a claim about an objective physical object, event, or state of affairs can be conclusively established by one observation or any finite number of observations. The main reason for this conclusion is the fact that any such statement has an indefinite number of consequences. For example, the statement, "There is a black telephone on the desk in front of me," implies that this object was constructed for the purpose of telephonic communication, that it contains certain kinds of equipment within it, that it will look like a telephone to most normal observers, that it will not vanish into thin air, etc. Whether or not this list of implications can be indefinitely extended, it is clear that we cannot by a single observation assure ourselves that all these implications are true. But if any one of the implications were false, then there would not be a telephone on the desk in front of me. Therefore, I cannot make sure that this statement is not false (that is, make sure that it is true) by a single observation. Therefore, no statement about objective, physical matters of fact can be an observation statement. This line of thought naturally leads to the position that the ultimate pieces of empirical evidence are "phenomenal statements," each of which is restricted to the claim that the observer's sensory experience was characterized in such and such a way, for example, "I seemed to see a black, telephone-shaped object." Purely subjective statements of this sort *can* be known with certainty on the basis of a single observation. They do not give rise to a multiplicity of independently testable implications. But having reached this rock bottom of certainty, it is difficult to get beyond it. Attempts to show how hypotheses concerning the physical world can be confirmed or disconfirmed by reference exclusively to "phenomenal data" have been unconvincing. Hence, many positivists have taken the position that whatever may be the case with "theoretical certainty," ordinary judgments of sense perception like "there is a telephone on my desk" have sufficient certainty to be taken as the ultimate evidence on which scientific testing rests. But even here, there are problems. Just what sorts of objective statements can be warrantably taken as conclusively established on the basis of a single observation? This problem becomes of practical importance in a science like psychology, where different schools differ in what they will recognize as empirical evidence. Psychoanalyti-

---

[10] Since we have seen how to extend the criterion to all sorts of sentences, we shall continue to discuss it in the more familiar form in which it is specifically applied to assertive sentences.

cally oriented clinical psychologists will take "He was very defensive," "He was extremely hostile," or "He tried hard to reassure me" as basic empirical data; whereas more hard-boiled "stimulus-response" psychologists will claim that these statements are themselves hypotheses that should, in principle, be tested in terms of such data as "He made very jerky movements," "His face was contorted," or "He uttered the sentence, 'Don't feel bad about it.'"

Second, there are problems over the kind of logical relations data must have to an assertion in order to count for or against it. These problems arise because of the fact that no nonobservation statement logically implies any observation statement by itself, but only in conjunction with other statements. For example, the nonobservation statement, "Ernest has intense unconscious hostility toward his father," will not by itself imply any statement reporting what would normally be taken to be a manifestation of such hostility, for example, "Ernest flared up at Mr. Jones." The latter will follow from the former only in conjunction with other premises, for example, "The repression is not so severe as to permit no expression," "Mr. Jones is perceived as sufficiently similar to Ernest's father to permit a displacement of the hostility onto him," and "The hostility has not all been worked off in other ways." Thus, the presence or absence of a given piece of data counts not just for or against one particular hypothesis, but rather for or against the whole body of premises used in deriving it. This makes the logic of confirmation rather complicated. Positivists have become aware that this makes it very difficult to exclude unwanted metaphysical statements. For such a statement can always be added to the premises yielding a given piece of empirical data in a way that makes it seem to be among the assertions that the data count for or against. Attempts to specify the logical relations involved so as to exclude this kind of maneuver have so far been unsuccessful.[11]

**Verifiability criterion as description and as proposal**

Let us suppose that we have the kinks out of the notion of an observation sentence and that we can specify the way in which a supposed assertion must be related to certain observation sentences in order that the evidence formulated in those observation sentences can be said to count for or against that assertion. We can finally come to the question: What can be said for or against accepting the verifiability criterion?

It is sometimes recommended on the grounds that it is simply a formulation of a criterion that, in fact, we always use in deciding what

[11] For an interesting account of these attempts, see C. G. Hempel, "Problems and Changes in the Empiricist Criterion of Meaning," in *Semantics and the Philosophy of Language*, ed. L. Linsky (Urbana, Illinois: University of Illinois Press, 1952).

does or does not make sense. However, unless the reference class of sentences (or the extension of 'we') is restricted in a question-begging way, this is palpably false. Positivists would never have made such a fuss over the criterion in the first place if it were not for the fact that the use of sentences that violate it is so widespread. Nor is this use restricted to professional philosophers. Utterances like 'God created the heavens and the earth,' which positivists take to be unverifiable, figure heavily in the discourse of the man in the street. It may be claimed that when people say things like this they are really confused, in that they are violating standards of meaningfulness to which they are firmly attached, and that by reflection on what they are doing, they could come to see that what they are doing is meaningless by their own standards. But nothing has been done to show that this is actually the case.

Most positivists have represented the theory as a *proposal* as to how the class of meaningful sentences should be delimited, rather than as an account of how it is, in fact, delimited. It may seem that once it takes on this form, the theory loses all pretension to being a criterion of meaningfulness. For it would seem that a given sentence is or is not meaningful (in a certain language community), whatever proposals we might make. Wouldn't proposing that certain sentences not be classed as meaningful be like proposing that certain bottles of milk not be classed as sour? If they *are* sour, then no proposal that we make is going to alter the matter. Of course, we could decide to change the meaning of the word 'meaningful.' But that would not make sentences that were meaningful in the usual sense not meaningful in the usual sense. And presumably it is meaningfulness in the usual sense in which we are interested, not meaningfulness in some sense that some group of philosophers sees fit to give it. However, this would be an insensitive way of viewing the situation. If we remember that 'meaningful,' like many terms, is markedly vague (see Chapter 5), we may realize that a proposal does not necessarily involve introducing a completely new sense. In fact, it is not clear on the face of it in every case just what we should regard as making sense. 'There is a telephone on the desk in front of me' clearly does make sense, and 'Green ideas sleep furiously' clearly does not. But if we simply reflect on the way we handle these clear cases, it is not easy to make explicit the principles on which we separate the sheep from the goats; it is still less easy to decide how we should, in terms of such principles, dispose of the kind of sentence illustrated by the list at the beginning of this chapter. Let us follow the theory of Chapters 1 and 2 and say that a sentence is meaningful if and only if it is usable for the performance of one or more illocutionary acts, and it is so usable if and only if its utterance is subject to certain kinds of rules. Having gone so far, we have still left certain questions dangling, in particular the question as to whether a sentence could be said to be governed by certain rules if the supposed rules stipulate conditions such that there is no empirical way of telling whether or not they hold. Thus, we may suppose that 'Every property inheres in a substratum' is subject to a rule that stipulates, among other things, that there are such entities as substrata. Let us grant that there is no empirical way of telling whether or not this is so. In this case, is the sentence really usable for performing an illocutionary act? Is it meaningful? It is not clear what we should say. We might well be pulled in both directions by our dispositions with respect to such words as 'meaningful.' Hence, there is a legitimate place for proposals as to how 'meaningful' can be made more precise.

**Arguments in support of verifiability criterion** What can be said by way of recommendation of this particular proposal? For one thing, the positivist can point to what happens when new theoretical terms are introduced into science. Consider the first introduction of the notion of unconscious desires, fears, guilt, etc. If we simply put the term 'hatred of one's father' together with 'unconscious' and let it go at that, it is hard to know what to make of the sentence, 'Ernest has an unconscious hatred of his father.' We know what to make of the statement that $x$ hates $y$ where there isn't this kind of qualification, and we know what it is to be unconscious of, say, the furniture in the room. But if all we have done is to take these terms with their established senses and combine them in this way, we have not given a sufficient indication of how this is to be taken. The most we have is a suggestion that the person in question might be thought of as hating his father (even though he really doesn't); we have what John Wisdom calls the expression of a "picture preference." In order to make clear what assertive force the sentence has, we would have to begin to specify how unconscious hatred would be manifested in observable behavior. It should not be expected that this would take the simple form of a hypothetical statement, specifying a certain kind of behavior as always contingent on unconscious hatred. We have to keep in mind the point made previously to the effect that a scientific hypothesis will entail a given observation report only in conjunction with other hypotheses and statements of observable conditions. Thus, when we begin to spell out connections, of the sort sketched on page 77, between the existence of unconscious hatred, degree of repression, relevant associations, and so forth on the one hand and observable behavior such as rudeness to an employer on the other, we have made a beginning at giving an assertive force to a sentence like 'Ernest has an unconscious hatred of his father.'

A similar point emerges from a consideration of what happens to an ordinary statement of fact if one begins to qualify it in such a way as to render it completely immune to any empirical disconfirmation. Consider the oft-cited parable of the gardener.

> Once upon a time two explorers came upon a clearing in the jungle. In the clearing were growing many flowers and many weeds. One explorer says, "Some gardener must tend this plot." The other disagrees, . . . So they pitch their tents and set a watch. No gardener is ever seen. "But perhaps he is an invisible gardener." So they set up a barbed-wire fence. They electrify it. . . . But no shrieks ever suggest that some intruder has received a shock. No movements of the wire ever betray an invisible climber. . . . At last the Sceptic despairs, "But what remains of your original assertion? Just how does what you call an invisible, intangible, eternally elusive gardener differ from an imaginary gardener or even from no gardener at all?" [12]

As this story suggests, what starts out as a genuine assertion will be reduced to a mere picture preference if we remove any possibility of putting it to an empirical test.

The question is: to what extent do these considerations show that sentences like those on our initial list do not make sense? [13] Let us consider a metaphysical philosopher who holds that properties like roundness and intelligence have a non-spatio-temporal mode of existence that is independent of their exemplifications. (There would still be such a thing as roundness even if there were no round things.) Call him a "Platonist." Our Platonist might make the following reply to the above arguments for the verifiability criterion.

"It is quite true that a supposed scientific principle, which is in principle untestable, is thereby debarred from consideration. But this is so because scientific hypotheses are constructed for the specific purpose of explaining and predicting observable phenomena; consequently, if a supposed scientific hypothesis has no connection with observation statements, it is not really a scientific hypothesis at all. Likewise, a supposed assertion about the physical world cannot be taken seriously unless it is possible to specify empirical tests. A physical state of affairs could not be objectively real unless it manifested itself in some way in sense experience. But this is because of what it is to be physical rather than because of what it is to make an assertion. We would not call anything 'physical' unless its existence would make some possible

---

[12] A. Flew, "Theology and Falsification," in *New Essays in Philosophical Theology*, eds. A. Flew and A. Macintyre (London: S.C.M. Press, 1955), p. 96. The idea is taken from J. Wisdom, "Gods," in *Logic and Language*, First Series, ed. A. Flew (Oxford: Basil Blackwell, 1952).

[13] We are assuming, for purposes of this discussion, that none of those sentences are empirically testable to any extent. This assumption is quite often made, but it has been challenged, especially in the case of sentence 1.

difference in the course of sense experience; hence, we would not take any utterance to be a genuine claim about the physical world unless it were possible to specify some empirical test of it. But it would be arbitrary in the extreme to extend these restrictions to assertions in general. In putting forward my metaphysical thesis, I am not making any claim about physical objects, events, or states of affairs, nor am I putting forward a hypothesis that has as its purpose the explanation or prediction of such matters. How could one reasonably hold these assertions, which are concerned with trans-physical matters, subject to the same restrictions? If there are such entities as properties existing independent of their exemplifications and an omnipotent spiritual creator of the physical universe, there would be no reason to expect them to manifest themselves in the details of our sense experience. (To suppose that we could formulate empirical tests for the thesis of the existence of God is to suppose that we could discern fixed regularities in the way in which God acts in the world; and a theist might well regard this idea as blasphemous.) Again, I could not expect my sense experience to be any different whether other people are really conscious, or whether they are simply intricate machines (provided the latter hypothesis allows for them being *very* ingeniously constructed). To adopt the verifiability criterion is to rule out even wondering whether such things are so; and it would seem that any principle that would prevent our recognizing the fact that a certain sort of thing exists is unreasonable. Thus, to show that a certain supposed assertion cannot be empirically tested is not to show that it is not an assertion; it is simply to show that it is a very different kind of assertion from scientific hypotheses and claims as to the nature of the physical world. And it is hardly surprising that metaphysics and theology should turn out to be very different from science."

It is hard to see what the positivist could say in rejoinder. He might say that the last point is not valid because one cannot talk intelligibly about the sorts of entities the metaphysician is claiming the positivists arbitrarily bars his talking about. But this claim could be supported only by recourse to the verifiability criterion, which is the very point at issue. Again, the positivist might ask the metaphysician how he proposes to determine, or even make a start at determining, whether his supposed assertions are true. Even if the metaphysician should admit that there is no way of showing that any one of these assertions is true, that in itself would not force him to admit to talking nonsense. That charge can be made to stick only if we can employ a wider version of a verifiability criterion, according to which assertive force is present only if there is some way, empirical or otherwise, of showing that what one says is true or false. But in any event, metaphysicians and theologians are rarely prepared to make any such admission. They usually think that there is some nonempirical way of showing that one or another metaphysical or theological position is correct. Thus, the Platonist metaphysician thinks that the objective existence of properties apart from their exemplifications can be established by a sort of intellectual nonsensory intuition of such entities, or perhaps by showing that their existence is a necessary presupposition of the use of language.[14] The positivist may maintain that the only way of really establishing any claim about matters of fact is the empirical way, but it is just as difficult to see how one can establish that claim as it is to see how one can establish the empirical verifiability criterion of meaningfulness. At this point, we may be at such a basic stratum of philosophical conviction that no basis can be found for argument. These are the convictions in terms of which arguments are given for lesser convictions.

**Final assessment** But perhaps something can be done to adjudicate the dispute. Recall the point made earlier that 'meaningful' is not a term with clearly defined boundaries. It is quite clear that 'My car is in the garage' does make sense, and equally clear that 'Quadruplicity drinks procrastination' does not make sense. But in between there is a border region where there are considerations that might well incline us in either direction. The positivist can at least claim that a sentence like 'Properties exist independent of their exemplifications,' which looks all right except for the absence of possible empirical tests, is defective in important respects. If it doesn't lead us, under any conceivable circumstances, to expect one sort of thing rather than another and if there is no way in which empirical investigation can throw any light whatsoever on its truth or falsity, then it is certainly not performing many of the functions we expect more typical assertions to perform; it is not a profitable subject of investigation in the way in which many assertions are. These considerations may or may not lead us to deny that the sentence makes sense. This will depend on the weight we give these sorts of considerations relative to others, for example, the meaningfulness of the components of the sentence, the correctness of the grammatical form, and the extent to which the sentence is logically related to a number of other (nonobservation) sentences, which also figure in discourse of this kind, for example, 'Not everything that exists is in space and time,' 'Nothing exists but particulars,' and 'Properties exist only in their exemplifications.' The important point is not that we should agree to tighten up the vague term 'make sense' in one direction

---

[14] See the quotation from Plato in the Introduction to this book.

rather than another, but that we should clearly see in just what ways a sentence that is not empirically testable is defective and in just what ways it is not. Having seen this, we shall know how it can and how it cannot be employed. And if we know that, labelling it 'meaningless' is of merely ritual significance.

# DIMENSIONS OF MEANING

5

Insofar as we achieve simple, clear-cut specifications of the meanings of words, we inevitably gloss over certain complexities. We have already seen how the multivocality of expressions (having more than one meaning) complicates talk about meaning. This is a relatively easy factor of which to take account, for we can simply give separate specifications of the various meanings of an expression and say something about the conditions in which it will be used in one or another sense. A semantic feature that is more difficult to handle is vagueness. Let us first get clear as to what vagueness is and then see how it complicates the semantic picture.

**What**
**vagueness is**
A term is said to be vague if there are cases in which there is no definite answer as to whether the term applies. 'Middle-aged' is vague in this sense. At age 5 and at age 80, one is not middle-aged; at age 50, one is. But what about 39, 41, or 60? There seem to be bands on either side of the clear cases of middle age where it is not clear what we should say. To say that there *is* no definite answer is not to say that we have not yet been able to give a definite answer because of insufficient evidence. The preceding point about 'middle-aged' is to be sharply distinguished from the fact that we are not able to say whether the term 'inhabited planet' is to be applied to Mars. In this case, we know reasonably well what kind of observations would lead to a positive or negative answer; it is just that, at present, we are not in a position to make those observations. But when we are unable to say whether a 41-year-old man is middle-aged, it is not because we have not yet made certain observations that would settle the question. It is not as if we

could decide this point by settling certain questions about the average blood pressure or metabolic rate of 41-year-old men. We have no idea what would definitely settle the question. It is not that we have not succeeded in finding the answer; there is no answer. This shows that the situation is due to an aspect of the meaning of the term, rather than to the current state of our knowledge.

The word 'vague' is commonly used very loosely (there is no inherent reason why 'vague' should be used loosely or even vaguely) to apply to any kind of looseness, indeterminacy, or lack of clarity. If we leave it in this condition, we shall run the risk of missing important distinctions. For example, we should distinguish vagueness, as just defined, from lack of specificity. If someone says, "We must take steps to meet this emergency," or if an advertisement reads, "It's the hidden quality that spells true value," people are likely to respond with "That's a very vague statement" or "Can't you be less vague?". However, the main difficulty here is not vagueness but lack of specificity. It is not that the word 'steps' is vague in that there are cases when it is not clear whether something should or should not be called a step; and it is not that there are cases where it can't be decided whether something is or is not a quality or is or is not hidden. (I am not denying that the words 'steps,' 'hidden,' and 'quality' are vague to some extent. I am saying that it is not the vagueness that attaches to these words that is primarily responsible for the insufficient determinateness of these statements.) The trouble lies in lack of specificity, in simply using the very general term 'steps' instead of spelling out some specific steps, and in using the very general term 'quality' instead of saying specifically which quality. We will be most likely to keep this distinction in mind if we restrict 'vague' to the definition given above. Of course, both vagueness and lack of specificity can attach in an important way to the same utterance, as in the advertisement, "Cash loans. Simple requirements." This is deficient both because of the failure to be specific as to what the requirements are and because of the vagueness of the term 'simple.' (Just how simple is simple?)

A more serious confusion is that between vagueness and metaphoricity. (People talk of "vague and metaphorical language.") We shall go into metaphor later in this chapter.

Another confusion that has infected many theoretical discussions is that between vagueness as a semantic feature of a term, which is what is specified by the above definition, and vagueness as an undesirable feature of a certain piece of discourse. This distinction is necessary because of the fact that vagueness in the first sense is not always undesirable. There are contexts in which we are much better off using a term that is vague in a certain respect than using terms that lack this kind of vagueness. One such context is diplomacy. Suppose the American ambassador to the U.S.S.R. is instructed to say "My government will strongly oppose any interference in the internal affairs of Hungary." This is vague because of the vagueness of the adverb 'strongly.' Just what constitutes *strong* opposition? Simply expressing disapproval in a press conference would clearly not be strong opposition, and declaring war clearly would be. But where in between is the line to be drawn? Is pressing for a UN resolution strong opposition? How about an economic embargo, open subsidization of anti-Russian elements in Hungary, or sending military "advisers"? The interesting fact is that there would be grave disadvantages in removing this vagueness. To commit ourselves definitely to opposition of a given degree of strength would sharply limit the range of alternatives open to us in a situation in which there may be a real strategic advantage in 1. keeping the opponent guessing and 2. choosing an alternative in the light of day-to-day changes in the situation. We *need* vague terms for situations like this.

There are also theoretical advantages to vagueness. Often our knowledge is such that we cannot formulate what we know in terms that are maximally precise without falsifying the statement or going far beyond the evidence. Thus, we have reason to think that city life imposes much more psychological strain on people than country life. However, in order to formulate this bit of knowledge, we have to use the vague term 'city.' (This word may receive precise definitions in certain legal contexts, but as ordinarly used it is not quite clear whether a community of 10,000 inhabitants is to be called a city.) This term can easily be made more precise by stipulating some minimum number of inhabitants, for example, 50,000. But as soon as we do so, we can no longer make the statement with any assurance. There is no precise population cutoff point such that there is a sharp difference in the psychological strain imposed by communities above and below this point.

Thus, when we use a word that has the semantic characteristic of vagueness, it may or may not be a liability. The failure to distinguish this semantic characteristic from defects of discourse to which it *may* give rise has led to an unfortunate transference of the negative evaluation of the latter to the former. Thinking about language has often been dominated by the unformulated and unexamined assumption that vagueness as a semantic characteristic is always undesirable and that an "ideal" language would contain no vague words.

This kind of distinction is less likely to be missed in the case of lack of specificity. It is tolerably obvious that to say that one word is more general than another is not to say that any utterance employing the former when the latter could have been used instead is going to suffer from lack of specificity in a pejorative sense. It seems obvious that sometimes we need a more rather than a less general term, because we want to say something general. A physicist who says "Metals expand when heated" rather than, for example, "Iron expands when heated" is unlikely to be excoriated for lack of specificity.

**Kinds of vagueness: degree and combination of conditions**

Thus far we have been concentrating on the kind of vagueness that involves the lack of a precise cutoff point along some dimension—age, number of inhabitants, or strength of opposition. This sort of vagueness furnishes the standard examples because it is the easiest to discern and to analyze, but it is by no means the only sort. Another, more complex source of indeterminacy in application can be found in the way in which a word can have a number of independent conditions of application. For a relatively simple example, consider 'fruit' in its culinary rather than biological sense, the sense in which it is contrasted with 'vegetable.' Thus, peaches, apples, bananas, and plums are clear cases of fruit, while lettuce, tomatoes, carrots, and spinach are clear cases of vegetables. It would seem that being a fruit in the biological sense, that is, being the part of the plant that bears the seeds, is involved in being a fruit in the culinary sense but is certainly not a sufficient condition, for many "vegetables" are fruits biologically, for example, tomatoes, beans, squash. If we add the requirement that fruit in the culinary sense be typically served in a sweetened form (in desserts, sweet drinks, etc.), then we can rule out the vegetables that are fruits biologically. We then have at least two "fruit-making" conditions, conditions each of which goes some way toward constituting something a fruit: 1. being a fruit biologically, and 2. being typically served in a sweet form, either because it is naturally sweet or because it has been sweetened. But just how are we to formulate a sufficient condition for the application of the term? We cannot say that anything satisfying either of the conditions is a fruit, for we have seen that many vegetables satisfy the first. We might say that anything satisfying both conditions is unquestionably a fruit, although it may be argued that it is not clear that a pumpkin, which satisfies both, is a fruit. The chief source of indeterminacy comes when we ask whether something is a fruit if it satisfies condition 2, but not condition 1. One example of this is rhubarb, which is always served in sweetened form but which is the stalk of the plant from which it comes. In fact, it is not clear how rhubarb is to be classified; this indeterminacy became of legal importance in Canada because of a law that levied different import duties for fruits and vegetables.

This humble example illustrates the kind of vagueness that stems from an indeterminacy as to just what combination of conditions is sufficient or necessary for the application of a term. We often have this kind of vagueness where there is a plurality of relevant conditions. Where all the conditions are satisfied, we have an ideally clear case. There will be some conditions, as in the preceding condition 1, the satisfaction of which is clearly not sufficient for the application of the term. But there will be some conditions and combinations of conditions such that when they are satisfied we do not know what to say, or we vacillate between one decision and the other, or mature native speakers of the language disagree. An important and complex example of this is the term 'religion.' If we try to list characteristic features of religion, features such that the possession of any of them does something to make that which has it a religion, we might come up with the following.

1. Beliefs in supernatural beings (gods).
2. A distinction between sacred and profane objects.
3. Ritual acts focused around sacred objects.
4. A moral code believed to be sanctioned by the gods.
5. Characteristically religious feelings (awe, sense of mystery, sense of guilt, adoration, etc.), which tend to be aroused in the presence of sacred objects and during the practice of ritual, and which are associated with the gods.
6. Prayer and other forms of communication with gods.
7. A world view, that is, a general picture of the world as a whole and of the place of the individual in it, including a specification of its over-all significance.
8. A more or less total organization of one's life based on the world view.
9. A social organization bound together by the preceding characteristics.

When a cultural entity exhibits all these features to a marked degree, we have an ideally clear case of religion, as with Roman Catholicism, Orthodox Judaism, Orphism.

We can say then that the conjunction of these features provides a sufficient condition for the application of the term 'religion.' But is it also necessary? What happens if one or more of these features is absent, or present only in an attenuated form? There are many cases of this sort. Ritual, and the demarcation of certain objects as sacred, can be sharply deemphasized, as in Protestantism and Islam. It can even drop out altogether, as with the Quakers and other groups who are mainly concerned with the cultivation of mystical experience. There are primitive societies where the moral code has no connection with the cultic system or the theology; moral rules are thought of as handed down from tribal ancestors rather than ordained by supernatural deities. Beliefs in supernatural beings can be whittled away to nothing, while leaving many of the other factors intact. Thus, in some Unitarian groups and in Humanism, we have a religiously toned orientation around certain ideals, such as social equality and a moral code based thereon, without the ardor being directed toward a supernatural being and without any cultus in which this ardor is expressed. One branch of Buddhism, the Hinayana, ignores supernatural beings, at least officially. The emphasis is on the cultivation of a moral and meditative discipline that will enable one to attain a state in which all craving has ceased. Finally, the social group can be reduced to one; that is, a person can develop his own private "religion." Spinoza, for example, worked out his own religion, which was based on a calm and joyful acceptance of everything that happened as necessarily flowing from the impersonal nature of the universe.

The important point is that with many combinations of these features we get uncertainty about and/or disputes over application of 'religion,' even when all the "facts" are agreed on. If we have all the features exemplified, we clearly have a religion; if none or almost none are exemplified, as with baseball, it is clearly not a religion. Anyone who disagreed with these judgments would thereby be showing that he did not understand the word 'religion.' But in between there will be several different sorts of cases in which the application of the terms is problematic. What are we to say about Humanism or Hinayana Buddhism or Communism? None of these systems have anything to do with personal deities. But Communism, for example, strongly exhibits other features; there is an elaborate cultus, sacred objects (for example, the body of Lenin, the works of Karl Marx), and a definite world view. It is just not clear what we should say. And if we go into a primitive society of the sort previously mentioned, are we going to say that the ritual system is the religion of the society, despite its dissociation from the moral code? And what if this ritual system involves no conception of personal deities? Again, it is not clear what to say, even if we have all the relevant facts about the society before us. A term like 'religion' gets its meaning through being applied to certain "paradigm" cases like Roman Catholicism; it is then extended to other cases that do not differ from the paradigm in too many respects. But it is impossible to say exactly how many respects are too many. (We should also note that it is not just a question of how *many* conditions are satisfied, for they are unequally weighted. As we ordinarily use the term 'religion,' the absence or near absence of beliefs in supernatural beings is more of a reason for denying application of the term than is the absence or near absence of ritual or the restriction to a single person. Presumably, this usage is connected with the fact that we live in a relatively nonritualistic culture.) Actually, 'religion' exhibits both kinds of vagueness. Even if we could say exactly which or how many of the various religion-making characteristics a cultural entity has to have in order to be a religion, we would be unable to say with respect to a given characteristic, exactly what degree of it we must have in order to apply the term. Many terms for cultural entities share this double vagueness.[1]

**Is absolute precision possible?** Is every word vague to some extent? Since there are contexts in which it is important to use language with as much precision as possible, this is a significant question. Quite often when one sets out to make a term more precise, it will turn out that the terms he employs to remove the vagueness in question will themselves be vague, though perhaps to a lesser degree and/or in different respects. Thus, if we try to remove the vagueness of the everyday word 'city' by stipulating that a community is a city if and only if it has at least 50,000 inhabitants, this removes the vagueness consisting in an indeterminacy as to the minimum number of inhabitants required; however, now the spotlight may be shifted to other areas of vagueness, for example, the term 'inhabitant.' Under what conditions is a person to be counted an inhabitant of a community? It is clear that a person who resides and works within the boundaries of a community is an inhabitant; and it is clear that one who has never set foot within it is not an inhabitant. But what if he owns a residence in the community that he occupies only in the summer, renting it out and living elsewhere the rest of the year? What if he attends college in the community, living in a dormitory while the college is in session but living outside the community while the college is not in session? What if he is living and working in the community for a fixed two-year period, but owns a home in another community which contains most of his belongings and to which he plans to return after this assignment is completed? Is he an inhabitant of the community during this two-year period? 'Community' is subject to a somewhat different sort of vagueness, which consists not in an indeterminacy as to what is to count as a community but rather as to what is to count as a single community. For political purposes, these questions are settled by legislation. The boundaries of a given community are established by law for matters of taxation, police authority, and eligibility to vote. But for other purposes—for example, sociological research—these boundaries may be of no importance. Thus, "a town" that straddles a state line may or may not be counted as a single community, depending on the questions at issue. Similarly, depending on the kind of problems at issue, Staten Island may or may not be counted as belonging to the same community as Manhattan Island.

---

[1] For a discussion along these lines of 'poem,' see C. L. Stevenson, "On 'What Is a Poem'?" *Philosophical Review*, LXCI (July 1957).

This example is instructive in several ways. First, it would be a serious mistake to suppose that we are making no progress but are simply replacing one example of vagueness with another. We have removed one element of vagueness—the indeterminacy as to the number of inhabitants required—and we have not *introduced* any *new* vagueness; rather by removing the first, we have made visible other vaguenesses that were there all along. Whatever vagueness attaches to 'inhabitant' automatically attaches to 'city,' whether or not we have definitely established how many inhabitants are required before we have a city. It is just that the indeterminacy over the number required is a more obvious feature and until that is removed we don't notice the problems as to what makes someone an inhabitant. Second, it is worthy of note that the problems raised about 'inhabitant' concerned the exact combination of conditions required for the application of the term, rather than a cutoff point along one or more dimensions, as with 'city.' Sometimes the residual vagueness will be of the sort removed, sometimes of a different sort, sometimes of both sorts.

The third point to be noted is that even if we could decide just which combination of conditions was necessary and sufficient for the application of the term 'inhabitant,' the terms in which these conditions are stated are themselves more or less vague. For example, we made use of the term 'works in the community.' No doubt, there are many cases in which the applicability or inapplicability of this term is unproblematic, but there are problematic cases as well. What of a salesman, the home office of whose company is in the community but who, by the nature of his work, spends most of his working hours elsewhere? Or, conversely, what of a man whose employer is elsewhere but who spends most of his working hours in the community in question, as a consultant or lobbyist? And what of a writer who happens to do most of his writing within the boundaries of the community? Does he "work in the community"? The term 'occupies a home' is also subject to vagueness. If a person owns several houses, does not rent any of them to others, and spends part of his time in each, does he occupy all of them or some one or more of them? And so it goes.

**Precision through quantification**    At this point we may feel that the removal of all vagueness from a given term is an unrealistic goal; the most we can hope to do is to approach it asymptotically. But before embracing that conclusion, we should consider the way scientists have tried to extricate themselves from the bog by replacing qualitative with quantitative terms. So long as we simply try to be more definite about the conditions of application without stating these conditions in terms of exact quantitative limits, as with our discussion of 'inhabitant,' it seems clear that we are going to wind up repeatedly with terms that are vague in one way or another. But if we do something like replacing 'hot' and 'cold' with numerical degrees of temperature, we may be able to do away with vagueness completely. We should not suppose, however, that the introduction of numbers is itself a panacea. The above discussion of 'city' suffices to show that. The introduction of a quantitative limit did not get rid of all vagueness, for the simple reason that we still had the problem of identifying the units to be counted. This problem arises for any activity of counting. In order to determine how many *P*'s there are, we have to be able to tell 1. when we have *P* rather than *Q*, and 2. when we have one *P* rather than more than one. Insofar as it is impossible to settle one or both of these questions, vagueness will attach to the numerical statement that there are so many *P*'s. Difficulty over 1 has been illustrated with 'inhabitant' and difficulty over 2 with 'community.' Both kinds of difficulty attach to many attempts to attain precision through specifying numbers of units required. Thus, we may try to remove the vagueness of "mountainous region" by requiring the presence of at least five mountains of 5,000 feet or over. But we run into the first problem in trying to decide whether we should say there are any mountains in a region that consists wholly of a plateau, the average elevation of which is 7,000 feet and which contains twelve noticeable elevations over the level of the plateau, ranging from 7,500 to 8,500 feet. The second problem emerges when we take something that is clearly a mountain range and try to divide it up into constituent mountains. Are two noticeable peaks divided by a saddle not very far below the height of the lower of the two peaks two mountains or only one? [2]

The introduction of measurements of positions along a continuum, as with length, temperature, and weight, is significantly different from the procedure of counting units specified with unreformed terms from ordinary language. If we replace 'large city lot' with 'city lot containing at least 20,000 square feet,' or replace 'cold drink' with 'drink, the temperature of which is 45 degrees F. or less,' we do not run into anything like the problems we encountered in counting inhabitants. Of course, we still have the problem of determining when we have a city lot, and when we have one city lot rather than two city lots; but there is no problem about identifying degrees of temperature or square feet, or about determining that at a given moment we are dealing with one

---

[2] This distinction between two problems cuts across the distinction already made between two kinds of vagueness. That is, a vagueness as to what counts as one *P*, as well as a vagueness as to when we have *P* rather than *not-P*, can be either of the *degree* or the *combination of conditions* sort. Our initial illustrations of the two kinds of vagueness were cases of vagueness as to when we have *P* rather than *not-P*. But by now we have examples of both kinds of vagueness with respect to the other sort of question. The point about 'community' exemplifies *combination of conditions* vagueness, and the point about 'mountain' exemplifies *degree* vagueness.

square foot rather than two. This, however, does not mean that indeterminacies of another sort might not emerge. Any measurement is reported subject to a certain margin of error. That means that we can never be absolutely certain that a lot boundary is exactly 100 feet— neither a fraction more nor a fraction less. (Though, of course, this measurement can be made in such a way that any uncertainty as may remain is of no practical importance.) This could be put by saying that '100 feet long' is vague to a certain extent, because in no situation are we ever absolutely certain that it is applicable. But this fact seems to be significantly different from those we have been discussing. This indeterminacy is due to inherent limitations on our powers of measurement, rather than to a feature of our language that might conceivably be altered in some other language. In other words, this uncertainty as to application is due to a certain insufficiency in the data (albeit an insufficiency that will never be remedied), rather than to a semantic feature of the words used. Each particular case of vagueness that we have considered can be removed by deciding to tighten up the criteria of application in a certain respect; but the indeterminacy stemming from the margin of error in measurements cannot be removed by any decision that is in our power to make. It seems best, then, not to regard this as a kind of vagueness, and to admit that in this one kind of case, at least, we have terms that are completely free of vagueness. But it must be remembered that it is only '200 square feet,' not 'city lot containing at least 200 square feet,' which has been declared vagueness-free. That is, any application of the nonvague measurement terms is going to exhibit whatever vagueness attaches to the terms we use to talk about whatever is being measured. This consideration is particularly important in the social sciences, where the use of precise measures is apt to mask the vagueness of the terms we use to specify what is being measured. Thus, we may get very precise looking results correlating degrees of prejudice toward Jews with degrees of acceptance of oneself. But the fact that we subject our data—for example, answers to questionnaires and clinical psychologists' ratings of responses to projective tests—to elaborate algebraic manipulations should not lead us to forget that in taking our final numerical results to give us degrees of acceptance of oneself, we are subject to all the indeterminacy that attaches to questions of the form, "Does Jones accept himself?"

**Open texture**     Friedrich Waismann, in his well-known essay, "Verifiability," [3] suggests that with respect to certain kinds of terms, particularly nouns denoting physical objects, there is a virtually inexhaustible source of vagueness, which will remain undisturbed after maneuvers of the

[3] In *Logic and Language*, First Series, ed. A. Flew (Oxford: Basil Blackwell, 1952).

preceding sorts. Waismann points out that apart from actual cases of indeterminacy of application, one can think of an indefinite number of possible cases in which one would not know what to say. He asks us to envisage the possibility that something to which we had been applying the word 'cat' with complete assurance should suddenly begin to speak, or should grow to the height of twelve feet, or should vanish into thin air and then reappear and vanish again from time to time. In such cases, we would not know whether to apply the term. Waismann also points out that a scientific term, like a word for a chemical element, 'gold,' which we would ordinarily think of as quite precisely defined, is in fact defined in such a way that we are prepared to take any one of several characteristics as conclusively showing that what we have is gold. These include the specific gravity, the spectrograph of light emitted when placed in a flame, the X-ray spectrum, and the ways it enters into chemical composition with other substances. Even if each of these criteria is quite precisely conceived, we can easily imagine a situation in which we would not know whether to apply the term 'gold,' namely, a situation in which some of the tests indicated gold and the others didn't. We might say that we use 'gold' subject to a presupposition that positive results on these tests will always go together, and that we use 'cat' subject to a presupposition that anything satisfying the ordinary criteria for something being a cat is not going to suddenly grow to a height of twelve feet, is not going to periodically vanish into thin air and reappear, and so on. The difference between these two cases is that the features Waismann mentions for 'gold' are quite explicitly involved in our ordinary use of the term, while the ones he brings out for 'cat' are not. We would never dream of making sure that an object does not disappear into thin air before saying that it is a cat. (This contrast holds for the things that Waismann said about 'gold' and 'cat,' rather than for these words themselves. We could undoubtedly parallel the point he made about 'cat' for 'gold' and vice versa.) The 'cat' case is the more important one, for no definite limit can be placed on the kind of conditions mentioned there. The number of wild situations we could envisage in which we would not know whether to say that what was before us was a cat is limited only by the extent of our ingenuity. As Waismann puts it, when we form a concept, we only have certain kinds of situations in mind; as a result, the concept is armed only against certain contingencies. This feature of a term Waismann calls "open texture," or "possibility of vagueness." His claim is that this kind of indeterminacy can never be completely eliminated; for although we can make a decision as to what we would say in any given kind of case, for example, vanishing into thin air and not reappearing, there will always be an indefinite number of other conceivable cases with respect to which the concept is still not delimited. It is not clear that it is, strictly speaking, impossible to decide all such cases in advance, for it is not clear just how numerous they are. But Waismann is surely justified in holding that, in fact, there will always be this kind of penumbra of indeterminacy attaching to physical object terms, and that in this they are to be distinguished from arithmetical terms, for example, with respect to which no such problems arise.

**Importance of the notion of vagueness**  Vagueness, like multivocality, can complicate specifications of meaning and identification of synonyms. For even if two expressions are perfectly synonymous on other grounds, they may differ in that one is vague in a respect in which the other is not. A relationship of this sort is what we are looking for when we try to make a term more precise; the hope is that, for example, 'drink with a temperature below 45 degrees F.' has exactly the same meaning as 'cold drink,' except that there is an indeterminacy in the latter that is absent in the former. But when we are trying to bring out the meaning of an expression as it actually is rather than polish it up, what we need is another expression that matches as exactly as possible the vagueness of the former. Thus, in defining 'adolescence' as *the period of life between childhood and adulthood,* we presumably have a good match. For the indeterminacy of the boundaries of adolescence is just the same as that which attaches to the upper boundary of childhood and the lower boundary of adulthood. There are many other places where vagueness should be, but often is not, taken account of. Thus, claims that a given statement is analytic (true solely in virtue of the meanings of the constituent terms) are liable to founder on the fact that the terms, though properly lined up in other respects, do not match with respect to vagueness. Thus, it may be claimed that "If someone lives in a city, he lives in a large community" is analytic. In adjudging this claim we should try to determine whether the vagueness of 'city' matches that of 'large community.' We should not suppose that it is possible to make any precise determination of this. It is characteristic of vague terms that there is no precise boundary between areas of clear application or non-application and areas of indeterminacy of application, any more than there are sharp boundaries between application and nonapplication. This is not surprising. It would be absurd to have the term 'city' sharpened to the point at which the area of indeterminacy of application is bounded precisely at, for example, 25,000 inhabitants and 40,000 inhabitants, without going farther and making a sharp boundary between application and nonapplication, that is, removing the area of indeterminacy altogether.

Vagueness should also be recognized in trying to give criteria of meaningfulness, like the verifiability criterion. Insofar as a term is vague, the question as to what evidence would confirm or disconfirm a statement asserting it of something does not have any precise answer. Thus, to recur to an earlier example, we can give no clear-cut answer to the question: "What evidence would confirm or disconfirm the thesis that there is no society without a religion?" For as we saw, in the face of certain collections of evidence, for example, a ritual system, a set of beliefs about spirits, and a moral code—none of which have any close connection with the others—it is, in principle, unclear whether we should say that the society has a religion.

Finally, the fact of vagueness forces us to make some sort of qualification in the supposedly self-evident "Law of Excluded Middle," that every statement is either true or false. For, as we have seen, where we have a borderline application of a vague term, it is, in principle, impossible to pronounce the statement either true or false. This will have to be handled either by qualifying the "Law," by denying that in these cases we really have a statement, or by saying that the Law holds only for a language in which all the terms are absolutely precise (and then what are we to say about languages that actually exist?).

**Metaphorical and other figurative uses of expressions**   Another thing that complicates the job of the semantic theorist is the fact of metaphorical uses of terms. After one recognizes the complications introduced by multivocality, he is still likely to think that one can give a complete account of the semantics of a language by specifying each of the senses of each of the words (or whatever is taken as minimum meaningful units), together with a set of recipes for deriving the meanings of larger units from the meanings of their elementary components plus the mode of combination. But even a complete system of this sort will not cover what is going on when e.e. cummings says: ˙

> the sweet small clumsy feet of april came into the ragged meadow of my soul

By any recognized method of distinguishing senses of terms, there is no sense of the word 'feet' in which we can speak of the feet of a month; nor is there any sense of 'meadow' in which a soul can have a meadow. Nor is cummings introducing new senses for them; what he says is intelligible to a reader only if that reader knows certain established senses of these words. The uses they have here are somehow parasitic on those established uses; they constitute a certain kind of extension of them. It is an extremely important fact about language that it is possible to use a word intelligibly without using it in any of its senses. There are other places in the philosophy of language where this fact has the effect of blurring sharp distinctions. 'Green ideas sleep furiously' is a common example of a meaningless sentence, one that is meaningless by reason of a "category mistake." (Ideas belong to the wrong category for being qualified by color terms.) But it is not at all difficult to imagine a poetic context in which this sentence would be quite appropriate, in which it could be used by the poet to communicate what he wanted to communicate. And so if we want the term 'meaningless' to preserve contact with 'uselessness for communication,' we must not say, unqualifiedly, that the sentence is meaningless, but only that it is meaningless in literal or prosaic discourse. And to the extent that such qualifications are necessary, it will be necessary to clarify the contrast between literal and figurative discourse.

Let us use the term 'figurative' in the following way. Wherever an expression is used so that, even though it is used in none of its established senses, nevertheless, what is said is intelligible to a fairly sensitive person with a command of the language, the expression will be said to be used figuratively. It is obvious that this sort of thing is possible only if these uses are somehow derivative from uses in established senses. Otherwise a knowledge of the standard senses would do nothing to enable a listener, however sensitive, to see what is being said. We can distinguish different kinds of figurative use in terms of the basis of derivation. Where the derivation is on the basis of a part-whole relationship, as when we say "The first ship opened fire" (it is a part of the ship that literally opened fire) or a genus-species relationship, as "I have not spoken to a single creature for a week" (that is, I have spoken to no men, a species of creature), one traditionally speaks of *synecdoche*. The term 'metonymy' has been used to cover cases in which the transfer is made on the basis of any one of a number of relationships, such as cause-effect, as when we say of a performer "He got a good hand" (that is, he got a lot of something produced by hands) or container-contained, as in "The White House had no comment." (None of these are figurative uses, as I have just defined that notion, because in all these cases the expressions in question are being used in established senses. These are examples of *figurative senses*. But they can serve as examples of kinds of basis of derivation.) Metaphor is that sort of figurative use in which the extension is on the basis of similarity. Consider the following passage from Shakespeare's Macbeth:

> MACBETH: *Methought I heard a voice cry "Sleep no more!*
> *Macbeth doth murder sleep," the innocent sleep,*
> *Sleep that knits up the ravell'd sleeve of care,*
> *The death of each day's life, sore labour's bath,*
> *Balm of hurt minds, great nature's second course,*
> *Chief nourisher in life's feast, . . .*
>
> Act II, scene ii.

It is because of some kind of similarity between what Shakespeare is attributing to sleep in the third line of the above quotation and what happens when one knits up a ravelled sleeve that one can understand what is being said, even though the words 'knit' and 'sleeve' are not being used in any established sense. Since metaphor is the most widespread and theoretically the most interesting of the figures of speech, we shall concentrate our attention on it. This treatment can, to a large extent, be transferred to the other figures of speech.

**The nature**    In his essay, "Metaphor," Paul Henle has given an illuminating
**of metaphor**    analysis, which employs Peirce's notion of an icon.[4] (See Chapter 3.) As pointed out previously, it is clear that in a metaphor one of the established senses of the expression is involved. This is clear, for unless one understands the relevant established sense, he will not be able to understand the metaphor. Unless one can understand sentences like "I knitted up the ravelled sleeve of that sweater," he will have no chance of understanding the third line of the above quotation. But one is not actually using the term in this sense; or, at least, one is not simply using it in this sense. One is somehow using the term to say something different, though related, and working *through* the established sense in order to do this. Although so much is abundantly clear, it is no easy task to give a precise specification of the mechanics of the operation. Henle suggests that we should think of the expression functioning in one of its established senses to specify a kind of object or situation that we are directed to use as an icon of what we are speaking about metaphorically.

> Metaphor, then, is analyzable into a double sort of semantic relationship. First, using symbols in Peirce's sense, directions are given for finding an object or situation. This use of language is quite ordinary. Second, it is implied that any object or situation fitting the direction may serve as an icon of what one wishes to describe. The icon is never actually presented; rather, through the rule, one understands what it must be and, through this understanding, what it signifies.[5]

On this analysis, to speak of sleep as knitting up the ravelled sleeve of care would be to say something like: "Consider a woman knitting up the ravelled sleeve of a sweater, and you will have an icon of the action of sleep on a careworn person." Instead of saying directly and explicitly what sort of effect sleep has on a careworn person, Shakespeare has presented us with another situation in which an agent is altering something in a certain specified way and is, in effect, suggesting that

[4] In P. Henle, ed., *Language, Thought, and Culture* (Ann Arbor, Mich.: University of Michigan Press, 1958).
[5] *Op. cit.*, p. 178.

by considering this situation we can realize something of the effect of sleep on a careworn person. But this is only possible if there *is* some important and readily noticeable similarity between the two situations; such similarity is a necessary condition of successful metaphor. If sleep had been apostrophized as that which "hammers nails into arrogance" we would not know what to make of it. This is not to say that metaphor is the same as simile, an explicit assertion of a similarity. In "The action of sleep on a careworn person is similar to the action of a knitter on a ravelled sleeve," no expression is used metaphorically. Nevertheless, it remains true that the existence of such a similarity is presupposed by the metaphor. Thus, the difference between metaphor and simile is somewhat analogous to the difference between 'My son plays baseball' and 'I have a son and he plays baseball,' where what is presupposed but not explicitly asserted in the first is explicitly asserted in the second.

We begin to see something of the pervasive importance of the capacity of language for figurative uses when we consider the phenomenon of "dead metaphor." The language is full of senses of terms that we can plausibly suppose, and in some cases even show by historical research, to have developed out of metaphorical uses of words. Consider such phrases as 'fork in the road,' 'leg of a table,' 'leaf of a book,' 'stem of a glass,' and 'eye lids.' In the present state of the language, the word 'fork' has as established a sense in this phrase as it does in the phrase 'knife and fork.' But we can well imagine that at an earlier time when the word was regularly applied only to the eating and cooking implement, people would use the word metaphorically in speaking of a place in which a road divided into two parts, each of which continues in roughly the same direction but making an acute angle with the line of direction of the original road. This use then "caught on," and because new generations could learn to apply the term directly to situations of this sort without needing to go through the older use, the sense in which the word is applied to roads came to be one of the established senses of the term. This example illustrates the very important role of metaphor in initiating uses of words that can eventually grow into new senses.

**Basis of the**
**literal—**
**metaphorical**
**distinction**

We have been putting a great deal of weight on the notion of an established sense of a term. The problem was presented as arising from the fact that words can be used intelligibly without being used in any established sense; and the account of metaphor given is such as to separate metaphorical uses of words from those uses in which the word is being used in a sense it actually has in the language. But how do we know that in 'He knit his brow,' 'knit' is being used in one of its established senses, whereas in 'Sleep knits up the ravelled sleeve of care,' it is not? One might object that the fact that the second sentence is so readily intelligible shows that the word is being used in a sense that a native speaker of the language would recognize it as having. On the other side, it can be pointed out that there are so many contexts of this sort that the project of listing a separate sense for each context would not recommend itself to the dictionary-maker as a feasible one. (And it may not be possible, in principle, to list all the contexts in which a word could be used intelligibly without being used in any of its commonly recognized senses.) But it may be said that although this is an important practical consideration for the practicing lexicographer, it does not decisively settle the theoretical question as to how many senses a word, in fact, has. To this it may be replied that it is a great mistake to suppose that there is any such thing as the number of different senses a word *really* has, independent of any considerations as to what is the most perspicuous way of *representing* its use in the language. However, it would be desirable to find some basis for refusing to distinguish separate senses for each metaphorical context, other than the difficulty of managing that many different senses. Perhaps we can find such a basis by considering the different ways in which what is being said on a given occasion can be explained to someone.

If someone does not understand what was said, the simplest way of bringing him to understand is to paraphrase the remark. The whole sentence can be paraphrased: when I said "Is that all right?" what I meant was "Will I be penalized for that?" Or the restatement may be confined to some component of the sentence, if it is clear that the failure to understand is concentrated at that point: "What do you mean, you've got a new case?" "By 'case' I mean *example*." This technique can be used with metaphorical utterances. Thus, I can explain 'Sleep knits up the ravelled sleeve of care' by saying, "That means that after a good night's sleep your cares and worries will not seem as pressing as they did before." But with utterances ordinarily regarded as metaphorical, this method is not as adequate as it is elsewhere. This kind of paraphrase fails to bring out the way in which what we are saying about sleep is based on the notion of someone repairing the sleeve of a garment by knitting. In bypassing the metaphorical extension, it thereby fails to bring out the richness of what had been said. Therefore, an explanation that explicitly brings out the comparison will be more adequate. "Just as in knitting up a ravelled sleeve one makes it whole again, restores it to its proper use, so when a careworn person gets a good night's sleep he is thereby restored to a condition in which he can function with normal effectiveness." (I am not suggesting that this is an ideally adequate or complete example of this type of explanation. The richer and more suggestive a metaphor is, the more impossible it is to spell out explicitly all the similarities that underlie it.) This will be more adequate because it not only makes clear what fact is being asserted concerning sleep but also makes explicit the way in which this fact is being asserted. Thus, we can use the necessity of this kind of explanation as a criterion of metaphorical use as opposed to use in an established sense. This fits in with the account given of metaphor. It is because the metaphorical use of an expression involves a double operation, in which we operate on the basis of an established sense but go beyond it, that the more elaborate explanation is needed.

What this criterion actually gives us is not a black and white distinction of kinds but a continuum of degrees. At one end, we have the clear cases of "literal" uses of terms, like "She is knitting a sweater." At the other end, we have clear cases of metaphors like "The sweet small clumsy feet of April came into the ragged meadow of my soul." Near the latter end, we have relatively standard metaphors like 'He blew his top,' 'Russia has dropped an iron curtain across Europe,' 'Religion has been corroded by the acids of modernity,' or 'He got into a stew,' where the frequency of sentences like this may lead one to distinguish a special sense of the word for such contexts. Thus, *Webster's New Collegiate Dictionary*, 1959 edition, lists as one of the senses of 'curtain': "anything that acts as a barrier or obstacle by protecting, hiding, or separating; as, a security *curtain*" (p. 204). And one of the senses listed for 'stew' is: *Colloq.* A state of agitating worry" (p. 831). Nevertheless, in each of these cases a more standard sense of the term is so clearly in the background that we are perhaps justified in feeling that one has not brought out the full force of what is being said unless one has made explicit the underlying comparison between, for example, the violent random motion of the meat and vegetables in a stew and the typical activity of a person who is "in a stew." Further down the scale toward literal meanings are the senses sometimes termed "figurative," such as the sense of 'cold' in 'He's a very cold person,' the sense of 'dead' in 'The socialist movement in this country is dead,' and the sense of 'hard' in 'hard liquor.' These are established senses, but very little reflection is needed to realize that they are derivative from more basic senses in the same sort of way as that in which a figurative use is derivative from use in an established sense. These senses can be separately specified; 'cold' in 'He's a cold person' means 'lacking in emotional expression.' Still, it seems that we would have some tendency to feel that a person who learned this just as a separate sense without seeing that to be cold in this sense is importantly like being at a relatively low temperature would be missing something. Still further down the scale will be what we earlier called "dead metaphors." Here there is little tendency to insist that one has not fully understood what one is saying when he speaks of a fork in the road unless he sees the similarity between this and a kitchen fork. The later sense has become almost completely autonomous. Nevertheless, the relation of derivation can be recovered on reflection; thus, we still have something that is distinguishable from senses so related, or unrelated, that we cannot discover even an archaic figurative derivation.

Until the last paragraph, I have succeeded in avoiding the term 'literal,' the usual contrast with 'metaphorical.' I have tried to avoid it because in the hands of the advocates of the verifiability theory, and other partisans of sweeping dichotomies, it has all but lost its usefulness. Originally, a literal use was one "according to the letter," which meant pretty much what I have been trying to convey by the term 'established sense.' But logical positivists began to use the term 'literal meaning' for what was countenanced by their criterion, and along with this they tended to use 'metaphorical,' 'emotive,' and 'poetic' indiscriminately for what was rejected by their criterion. Such usages only spawn confusion. There is even less justification for the phrase 'literal meaning' than for the phrase 'cognitive meaning' or 'factual meaning.' A term can be said to be *used* literally when it is used in such a way that the meaning of the sentences in which it occurs is a determinate function of one of its senses. It is a mistake, however, to think that 'literal' denotes a *kind* of meaning. As should be clear from the above account, whenever we use an expression with an assignable meaning we are using it literally. Thus, all meanings would be "literal"; the term as so used has no distinguishing power. The confusion thickens when it is supposed that "literal meaning" is empirically respectable meaning, as opposed to what is indifferently labelled "emotive meaning" or "metaphorical meaning." Quite apart from the confusion involved in using these terms to mark "kinds of meaning," there is no justification for regarding a metaphorical statement as ipso facto unverifiable. It is true, of course, that when one is speaking metaphorically, it is generally more difficult to be sure of exactly what he is saying than when he is speaking literally. In effect, he has given us something as a model for something else without making explicit in exactly what way it is supposed to be a model; we have lost the controls that come from using words in established senses. But this simply means that what he is saying is, to a certain extent, indeterminate, just as it is if the expressions he uses are vague. It does nothing to show that what he is saying, insofar as one can be sure of what it is, cannot be put to an empirical test; and still less does it show that what he is saying is distinctively "emotive." When I say "Sleep knits up the ravelled sleeve of care," to a large extent I am saying the same thing one would normally say in uttering the sentence,

'As a result of getting a good night's sleep a careworn person will be less disturbed and distracted by his cares.' And to the extent that it can be determined that I am saying the same thing, there is no difficulty in seeing what sorts of observations would confirm or disconfirm what I am saying. There are, however, many metaphorical statements for which it is difficult to imagine any empirical test, for example, "Life's . . . a poor player that struts and frets his hour upon the stage and then is heard no more." But this is not because the statement is metaphorical. If we take an approximate literal paraphrase, for example, "Life is futile," we will have the same kind of difficulty in imagining an empirical test for it. Although it may be the case that empirically untestable statements often assume a metaphorical form, it is not the fact that they are expressed metaphorically that makes them untestable.

**Irreducible metaphors: God and inner feelings**     We have briefly considered the topic of dead metaphors. A class of metaphors that is of special interest philosophically is made up of those that cannot die. They are importantly involved in theology and in descriptions of feelings. To see that this is so, we shall have to go more deeply into the distinction between the words 'literal' and 'metaphorical' than we did previously.

Thus far we have rested the literal-metaphorical distinction on the notion of established senses of an expression, without looking very far into what is involved in a sense becoming established. If we accept uncritically the usual lexicographical procedures, there is no doubt that, on the account of the literal-metaphorical distinctions that we have been giving, the following statements involve literal rather than metaphorical uses of words.

1. God made the heavens and the earth.
2. God spoke to the prophets in days of old.
3. God has punished me for my sins.
4. I felt a stabbing pain.
5. When I heard the news, I was transported.
6. I felt constricted.
7. When I hear that music, I get the feeling of marching along in a triumphal procession.

With respect to the feeling terms, this is so because we have used 'stabbing,' for example, so often in application to pains, that by the usual lexicographical criteria one is justified in distinguishing a separate sense. As for the theological contexts, it is not that special senses are involved; rather, senses are specified in such a way as to cover application both to man and God. Thus, one of the senses of 'make' in *Webster's New Collegiate Dictionary* is "To cause to exist, appear, or occur" (p. 507), and one of the listings for 'punish' is "to afflict with pain, loss, or suffering for a crime or fault" (p. 685). Nevertheless, it is a very important fact that some of these established senses (or, alternatively, some of the uses of these established senses) are related to others in a way similar to that in which metaphorical uses are related to literal uses. This begins to appear if we ask how we would explain to someone what is meant by "God has punished me" and by "My father has punished me." It is a striking fact that although the latter can, in principle, be explained by directing the learner's attention to certain observable transactions, the former can be explained only by directing the learner to take cases of one man punishing another as models (or icons) of what is meant, much as a clearly metaphorical statement directs the listener to take a certain kind of situation as a model of something else. This priority is necessary and irreversible. There is no way of explaining what it is for God to punish someone other than by saying, in effect, that it is something like one man punishing another, for it is impossible to use anything like the "ostensive" teaching device usable for 'My father punished me.' Whether or not a person can be aware of God punishing him need not be decided in order for us to make our point. Ostensive teaching is impossible here because it is impossible for the teacher to tell *when* the learner is aware of God punishing him (unless the learner can tell him that he is so aware; but in that case, the "learner" has already learned his lesson in some other way). For divine punishment, there is nothing analogous to the publicly observable direction of visual attention that shows the teacher when the learner is paying attention to an act of human punishment. Furthermore, it is impossible to define 'God punished me' in any terms that are not analogically derivative from talk of human activity. I do not have the space to justify this last claim, for that would involve going through all the possible sorts of definition that seem initially plausible; the reader is invited to try any verbal explanations of the sentence he can think of and see what happens. Let us take a brief look at one possibility. It may be said that 'God punished me' means 'God caused me to suffer as a result of my doing something wrong.' This latter sentence may be acceptable as an equivalent, but the fact remains that 'cause' in this context raises exactly the same problems as 'punish.'

We do not have to rely on so controversial an area of discourse as theology for examples of this phenomenon. The point can be amply illustrated from our talk about feelings and sensations. There are some feeling and sensation terms that can be intersubjectively stabilized by reference to more or less constant situational or behavioral concomitants. These include 'pain,' 'depressed,' 'excited,' and 'sleepy.' But our talk about feelings and sensations is by no means confined to these terms. If we consider the terms we use to distinguish one kind of pain from another, we shall find it impossible to tie them down in this way. If we want to explain to someone what a stabbing pain is, as opposed to a dull ache or a burning pain, we shall be forced back to analogy. A stabbing pain is one that is like the pain one would receive if he were stabbed. There is no other way to make explicit the meaning of the expression. And to express our feelings with any fineness of detail, we must use many terms that depend on analogies for their significance. There is no publicly observable situational feature, facial expression, or behavior that is specially tied to feeling constricted, as contrasted with feeling embarrassed, apprehensive, or out of place. Again, it seems that one can explain the term only by saying that to feel constricted is to feel something like the way one feels when he is physically constricted. Let us use the term 'quasi-metaphorical' for senses or uses of words that can, in the last analysis, be explained only by analogy with what is talked about when these or other words are used in senses that can be explained more directly.

Quasi-metaphors are, in the epistemologically crucial respects, in the position of metaphors that cannot die. They have the characteristic indeterminacy of metaphors, but they lack the means, available for many metaphors, for removing this indeterminacy. As we have seen, a metaphor in the raw simply consists of specifying a model or icon for something without specifying the respects in which it is an icon. Nevertheless, in many cases there are devices for removing, or at least sharply reducing, this indeterminacy. Sometimes we can point out examples of what we are talking about and leave the hearer to see for himself what the relevant similarity is. In other cases where, owing to the abstractness or pervasiveness of the subject matter, this cannot be done, we can give at least an approximate paraphrase in literal terms, as in the preceding treatment of 'Sleep knits up the ravelled sleeve of care.' But in a quasi-metaphor, as we have defined that term, neither of these devices is available. We cannot point to cases of God punishing someone or to cases of someone feeling constricted; even if we could point to such cases, doing so would do nothing toward helping someone realize what features of human punishing and physical constriction are being carried over into these concepts. And we cannot give paraphrases of 'God has punished me' or 'I feel constricted' in terms that do not themselves involve quasi-metaphors. This means that the indeterminacy characteristic of metaphors is indelibly stamped on these areas of our talk. It is not clear either exactly what we are saying or what would be required to confirm or disconfirm it. Concentration on statements of this sort is perhaps partly responsible for the mistaken view that metaphorical statements are inherently untestable. (There may well be other reasons why theological statements, in particular, are refractory to empirical test; the present point is that, apart from other reasons, empirical testing is made difficult because of this kind of ineradicable indeterminacy.) These considerations have led logistically and positivistically minded philosophers to become extremely impatient with these modes of discourse. They have typically favored complete annihilation for theology and replacement of our ordinary talk about feelings with "physicalistic" talk about states of the nervous system. Without going this far, we can at least point out that philosophers of religion and philosophers of mind should give more attention to the semantic status of the quasi-metaphorical terms in their domains than they have done to date.[6]

[6] For a detailed discussion along these lines of the status of theological terms, see W. P. Alston, "The Elucidation of Religious Statements," in *The Hartshorne Festschrift: Process and Divinity*, ed. William L. Reese and Eugene Freeman (La Salle, Illinois: Open Court Publishing Co., 1964), pp. 429-443.

Because of limitations of space, I have omitted from this bibliography any works referred to in the course of the book. Thus, the reader can skim the footnotes for additional suggestions.

CHAPTER 1

The more sophisticated versions of the reference theory of meaning are to be found in the writings of logicians. These range from the nineteenth century logicians, J. S. Mill, A *System of Logic*, Bk. I (London: Longmans, Green & Company, Ltd., 1906) and Gottlob Frege, "On Sense and Reference," in *Philosophical Writings*, ed. Peter Geach and Max Black (Oxford: Basil Blackwell, 1952), to the more contemporary treatments of Alonzo Church in "The Need for Abstract Entities in Semantic Analysis," *Proceedings of the American Academy of Arts and Sciences*, 80 (1951) and C. I. Lewis, "The Modes of Meaning," in Leonard Linski, ed., *Semantics and the Philosophy of Language* (Urbana, Illinois: University of Illinois Press, 1952). Rudolf Carnap has pursued this kind of approach by constructing elaborate logical systems in *Introduction to Semantics* (Cambridge: Harvard University Press, 1942) and in *Meaning and Necessity* (Chicago: University of Chicago Press, 1947). Modern refinements of the ideational theory of meaning include C. L. Stevenson's formulation in terms of dispositions of linguistic expressions to produce psychological effects in hearers, in Chapter 3 of *Ethics and Language* (New Haven, Conn.: Yale University Press, 1944) and a formulation in terms of intentions of speakers to produce psychological effects in hearers, in Unit 14 of Henry Leonard's *An Introduction to Principles of Right Reason* (New York: Holt, Rinehart & Winston, Inc., 1957) and in H. P. Grice's "Meaning," *Philosophical Review*, 66 (1957). An historically important source for the stimulus-response theory is Chapters 3 and 9 of C. K. Ogden and I. A. Richards, *The Meaning of Meaning*, 5th ed. (New York: Harcourt, Brace & World, Inc., 1938).

Bloomfield's theory undergoes some refinement and elaboration in C. C. Fries, "Meaning and Linguistic Analysis," *Language*, 30 (1951). Paul Ziff, *Semantic Analysis* (Ithaca, N. Y.: Cornell University Press, 1960) and W. V. Quine, *Word and Object* (New York: John Wiley & Sons, Inc., 1960) represent divergent but equally sophisticated developments of the notion that the meaning of an expression is a function of the conditions under which it is uttered. B. F. Skinner's *Verbal Behavior* (New York: Appleton-Century-Crofts, Inc., 1957), represents the most determined attempt to apply stimulus-response concepts to language; and even though he explicitly eschews use of semantic terms, his programme has clear implications for their analysis. Chapter 3 of Roger Brown's *Words and Things* (New York: Free Press of Glencoe, Inc., 1958) provides a useful review of stimulus-response theories, and Chapter 7 of Max Black's *Language and Philosophy* (Ithaca, N. Y.: Cornell University Press, 1949) is a penetrating discussion of Morris' account of signs.

CHAPTER 2

Paul Feyerabend's "Wittgenstein's Philosophical Investigations," *Philosophical Review*, 64 (1955) presents one interpretation of Wittgenstein's philosophy of language. All of the essays collected in *Ordinary Language*, ed. V. C. Chappell (Englewood Cliffs, N. J.: Prentice-Hall, Inc., 1964) throw light on the sense in which contemporary philosophers are concerned with the ordinary *use* of linguistic expressions. Good examples of standard treatments of "uses of language" can be found in Chapter 2 of I. M. Copi's *Introduction to Logic*, 2nd ed. (New York: The Macmillan Company, 1961), and in William Frankena, "Some Aspects of Language" and "'Cognitive' and 'Non-Cognitive,'" in Paul Henle, ed., *Language, Thought, and Culture* (Ann Arbor, Michigan: University of Michigan Press, 1958). An elaborate discussion of the nature and varieties of definition is to be found in Part IV of Henry Leonard's *An Introduction to Principles of Right Reason* (New York: Holt, Rinehart & Winston, Inc., 1957). For stimulating discussions of problems connected with the notion of synonymy see Nelson Goodman, "On Likeness of Meaning" and Benson Mates, "Synonymy," both reprinted in Leonard Linsky, ed., *Semantics and the Philosophy of Language* (Urbana, Illinois: University of Illinois Press, 1952).

CHAPTER 3

Chapters 4-6 of H. H. Price, *Thinking and Experience* (London: Hutchinson's University Library, 1953) are very good on the distinction between signs and symbols. Interesting discussions of the varieties of symbolism include Suzanne Langer, *Philosophy in a New Key* (New York: New American Library, 1948), Part II of W. M. Urban, *Language and Reality* (New York: The Macmillan Company, 1939), and Philip Wheelwright, *The Burning Fountain* (Bloomington, Indiana: University of Indiana Press, 1954). For useful discussions of the nature of language see Chapter 1 of Edward Sapir, *Language* (New York: Harcourt, Brace & World, Inc., 1921), Chapter 2 of J. B. Carroll, *The Study of Language* (Cambridge, Massachusetts: Harvard University Press, 1955), and Chapter 1 of A. A. Hill, *Introduction to Linguistic Structures* (New York: Harcourt, Brace & World, Inc., 1958).

CHAPTER 4

The spirit of the traditional empiricism of Locke and Hume lives on in C. I. Lewis and H. H. Price. For Lewis, see Book I of his *Analysis of Knowledge and Valuation* (LaSalle, Illinois: Open Court Publishing Co., 1946). For Price, see *Thinking and Experience* (London: Hutchinson's University Library, 1953). The Bible of logical atomism was Ludwig Wittgenstein's *Tractatus Logico-Philosophicus* (New York: Harcourt, Brace & World, Inc., 1922). For an excellent critical review of the movement see J. O. Urmson, *Philosophical Analysis, Its Development Between the Two World Wars* (Oxford: The Clarendon Press, 1956). Many of the classic papers of the logical positivist movement are collected in A. J. Ayer, ed., *Logical Positivism* (New York: Free Press of Glencoe, Inc., 1959). For readily intelligible expositions of the verifiability criterion plus many applications to philosophical problems see Rudolf Carnap, *Philosophy and Logical Syntax* (London: Psyche Miniatures, 1955) and A. J. Ayer, *Language, Truth, and Logic*, 2nd ed. (London: Victor Gollancz, Ltd., 1946). For recent restatements of the verifiability criterion see C. G. Hempel, "The Concept of Cognitive Significance: A Reconsideration," *Proceedings of the American Academy of Arts and Sciences*, 80 (1951) and, with special reference to the application of the criterion to scientific theories, Rudolf Carnap's essays, "Testability and Meaning," reprinted in Herbert Feigl and May Brodbeck, eds., *Readings in the Philosophy of Science* (New York: Appleton-Century-Crofts, Inc., 1953) and "The Methodological Character of Theoretical Concepts," *Minnesota Studies in the Philosophy of Science*, Vol. I (Minneapolis: University of Minnesota Press, 1956). Important criticisms of the verifiability criterion are to be found in A. C. Ewing, "Meaninglessness," *Mind*, 46 (1937) and in G. J. Warnock, "Verification and the Use of Language," *Revue Internationale de Philosophie* (1951).

CHAPTER 5

Important treatments of vagueness can be found in Max Black, "Vagueness: An Exercise in Logical Analysis," in *Language and Philosophy* (Ithaca, N. Y.: Cornell University Press, 1949) and in Chapter 4 of W. V. Quine, *Word and Object* (New York: John Wiley & Sons, Inc., 1960). Stimulating discussions of metaphor include Chapters 5 and 6 of I. A. Richards' *The Philosophy of Rhetoric* (London: Oxford University Press, 1936), Chapter 6 of Philip Wheelwright, *The Burning Fountain* (Bloomington, Indiana: Indiana University Press, 1954), and Max Black, "Metaphor," in *Models and Metaphors* (Ithaca, N. Y.: Cornell University Press, 1962). Monroe Beardsley's "The Metaphorical Twist," *Philosophy and Phenomenological Research*, 22 (1962) contains an acute criticism of the view presented in this book, as well as the development of an alternative position.

# INDEX